D0627855

UNIX in a Nutshell
Berkeley Edition

UNIX in a Nutshell

Berkeley Edition

A Desktop Quick Reference

O'Reilly & Associates, Inc.
103 Morris Street, Suite A
Sebastopol, CA 95472

UNIX in a Nutshell Berkeley Edition

Editor: Tim O'Reilly

The following staff members of O'Reilly & Associates, Inc., worked on this book: Jean Diaz, Dale Dougherty, Daniel Gilly, Linda Mui, Tim O'Reilly, Thomas Van Raalte,Linda Walsh, Sue Willing, and Donna Woonteiler. Special thanks to Cathy Brennan and Jill Berlin.

Printing History:

December 1986:	First edition.
September 1987:	Minor corrections.
April 1989:	Minor corrections.
November 1989:	Minor corrections.
October 1990:	Minor corrections.

This book is printed on acid-free paper with 50% recycled content, 10-15% post-consumer waste. O'Reilly & Associates is committed to using paper with the highest recycled content available consistent with high quality.

ISBN: 0-937175-20-X   [8/92]

TABLE OF CONTENTS

1 UNIX Commands

2 Shell Syntax

3 Pattern Matching

4 Editor Command Summary

5 Nroff and Troff

6 Macro Packages

7 Preprocessors

8 Program Debugging

9 SCCS and Make

UNIX in a Nutshell

1

UNIX Commands

This section includes a description of each command found in Section 1 of the *UNIX Programmer's Manual*. The command syntax is followed by a brief description of the command's function and a list of all available options, as described in Releases 4.2 and 4.3 of Berkeley UNIX.

The conventions used in this section are as follows:

- All commands and options shown in **boldface** are typed literally.

- All arguments and options shown in *italics* are generic and should be replaced with user-supplied values.

- All arguments surrounded with brackets are optional. Note that many commands show the argument [*file(s)*]. If a filename is omitted, standard input (i.e., the keyboard) is assumed. End with an EOF character (normally ^D).

- The syntax line should be entered as shown, including blank spaces. Note, for example, that an option shown as -w*n* (the numeric argument *n* follows the -w flag with no intervening whitespace) is different from -w *n*.

- A ☞ at the bottom of a right-hand page means that the listing for the current command is continued on the next page.

adb

adb [*options*] [*objfile* [*corefile*]]

A general purpose debugging program used to look at **core** files resulting from aborted programs. *objfile* contains an executable program and *corefile* contains the core image produced when *objfile* is executed. **a.out** is the default *objfile*. **core** is the default *corefile*. See Section 8 for more information on **adb**.

options

    -w   create both *objfile* and *corefile* and open for modification.

    -k   perform UNIX kernel memory mapping.

    -I*dir* specify directory *dir* where files will be read from (default is **/usr/lib/adb**).

addbib *bib*

addbib [*options*] *database*

Interactively create or add bibliographic information to *database*. See also **refer**.

options

    -p *pfile*

        use *pfile* as the template for the interactive prompts. *pfile* must contain the new prompt strings followed by a TAB and the keyletters to be inserted in *database*.

    -a   suppress prompting for input.

admin *sccs*

admin [*options*] *files*

Add *files* to SCCS or change *options* of SCCS *files*. See also **sccs**; for more information on SCCS, see Section 9.

options

    -a*user*|*groupid*

        assign *user* or *groupid* permission to make deltas.

    -d*flag* delete *flag*. Values are:

        b   allow branch deltas.

        c*n*   set highest release to *n* (default is 9999).

f*n*	set lowest release to *n* (default is 1).	**admin** *continued*

f*n*	set lowest release to *n* (default is 1).
d*n*	set **get** default delta number.
i	treat "No id keywords (ge6)" as a fatal error.
j	allow multiple concurrent **gets**.
l*list*	releases in *list* cannot accept changes.
n	create a null delta.
q*string*	substitute %Q% keyword with *string*.
m*name*	substitute %M% keyword with module *name*.
t*type*	substitute %Y% keyword with module *type*.
v[*file*]	prompt for modification request number as the reason for creating a delta.

-e*user*
> take away delta privileges from *user*.

-f*flag*[*value*]
> set *flag* with optional *value*. Allowable flags and values are the same as described for -d*flag* above.

-h check the SCCS file structure.

-i[*file*]
> use *file* as source.

-m[*list*]
> insert *list* of modification request numbers.

-n create a new SCCS file.

-r*n.n* set initial delta to release number *n.n*.

-t[*file*]
> take descriptive text from *file*.

-y[*text*]
> insert *text* as comment for initial delta (only valid with -i or -n).

-z recompute the SCCS file checksum and store in first line.

---

apply [*options*] *command arguments*

Run the named *command* on each *argument* in succession.

apply
continued

options

    -ac   specify command character *c* (default is %).

    -n   process *n* arguments per command (default is 1). If *n* is 0, run *command* without arguments. Optional arguments are an ascending integer sequence which causes *command* to be repeated the number of times specified by the highest integer.

command

In *command*, the character string %*d*, where *d* is a digit from 1 to 9, is replaced by the *d*th unused argument following the command.

---

apropos

apropos *keywords*

Print the sections of the *UNIX Reference Manual* that contain one or more *keywords* in their title. Synonym for **man -k**.

---

ar

ar *key* [*posname*] *archivefile files*

Maintain a group of *files* that are combined into *archivefile*.

key

    a   after *posname* (used with **r** or **m**).
    b   before *posname* (used with **r** or **m**).
    c   create *archivefile* silently.
    d   delete *files* from *archivefile*.
    i   before *posname* (used with **r** or **m**).
    l   place temporary files in local directory rather than /**tmp**.
    m   move *files* to end of *archivefile*.
    p   print *files* in *archivefile*.
    q   append *files* to *archivefile*.
    r [**u**]   replace *files* or, with the **-u** flag, only files modified later than *archivefile*.
    t   print table of contents for *archivefile*.
    v   verbose, print a description.
    x   extract *files* from *archivefile*.

posname	**ar**
Name of a file used to indicate the position in *archive-file*. Must be preceded by: **a**(after), **b** or **i** (before).	*continued*

---

as [*options*] [*file* ...]   **as**

VAX-11 assembler of named file or of standard input (default).

options

-a*n*   specify the alignment of procedures and data blocks to be 2^n (default $= 2^2 = 4$). $1 \leq n \leq 16$.

-d*n*   specify the number of bytes to be assembled for offsets of normally indeterminate size, which involve external or forward references. *n* can be **1, 2,** or **4** (default).

-J   use long branches to resolve jumps in cases where byte-displacement branches are insufficient.

-L   save defined labels beginning with "L."

-o *objfile*
    send assembly output to *objfile* (default file is **a.out**).

-R   make initialized data segments read-only.

-t *directory*
    the temporary file is sent to *directory* instead of default **/tmp**.

-V   use virtual memory, rather than a temporary file, for some intermediate storage.

-W   do not send error messages.

---

at [*options*] *time* [*date*] [*file*]   **at**

Execute commands located in *file* at a specified *time* and optional *date*. If *file* not specified, read commands from standard input; end with ^D.

options

-c   use *csh* to execute the program.

-s   use *sh* to execute the program.

-m   send mail to user to verify that job is completed.

☞

at *continued*	*time* hour (hh), minute (mm), and optional a(am), p(pm), m(midnight), or n(noon) (e.g., *8a, 1530*). *date* month name followed by a day number (e.g., *jan 24*) or a day of the week (e.g., *jan mon*). Add the word "week," and the command is executed a week later (e.g., *jan mon week*).

atq	**atq** [*options*] [*name*]
	
	Print jobs created by the **at** command which are still in the queue. Jobs are normally sorted by when they will be executed.
	options
	    -c sort the queue by the time the **at** command was given.
	    -n only print number of files in the queue.

atrm	**atrm** [*options*] [[*n*] *user*]
	
	Remove jobs created by the **at** command belonging to *user*. *n* is the optional job number.
	options
	    - remove all jobs belonging to user invoking **atrm**.
	    -f suppress all information regarding removal.
	    -i interactive removal; prompt user for verification before each removal.

awk	**awk** [*options*] [*program*] [*files*] Use the pattern-matching *program* to modify the specified *files*. See Section 3 for details on pattern-matching. See Section 4 for more information on **awk**. *options* **-** read standard input for patterns.

-ffile	use patterns contained in file.	**awk**
-Fc	separate fields with character c.	continued

---

basename pathname [suffix] **basename**

Remove the path prefix and optional suffix (e.g. .c) from pathname and print the resulting filename on standard output. See also **dirname**. 2→ when?

---

bc [options] [files] **bc**

Perform precision arithmetic interactively. Input is taken from files or read from the standard input.

options

    -c   do not invoke **dc**, compile only.
    -l   use arbitrary precision math library.

---

bib [options] bib **bib**

Format citations and bibliographies for nroff and troff.

options

    -aa   abbreviate authors' first names
    -ar[n] reverse the names of the first n authors, or of all authors if n is omitted.
    -ax   print authors' names in caps/small-caps style.
    -ctemplate
            build citations according to template.
    -ea   abbreviate editors' first names.
    -ex   print editors' names in caps/small-caps style.
    -er[n] reverse the names of the first n editors, or of all editors if n is omitted.
    -f   dump references immediately following citation line.
    -ifile process formatted file.
    -h   hyphenate adjacent reference items (e.g. "6,7,8,9" becomes "6-9"). (Implies the **-o** option.)
    -nstring
            Turn off options in string, string consisting of **a**, **f**, **h**, **o**, **s**, and **x**.

---

bib *continued*	**-o** order contiguous citations before printing (default). **-p***files* search *files* before searching the system file. *files* is a comma-separated list created by **invert**. **-s***template* sort references according to *template*. **-t***type* use standard macros and switch settings of *type*.

biff	**biff** [y|n]
	
	Notify the user when mail arrives during the current login session.
	   y enable notification.
	   n disable notification.

cal	**cal** [*month*] *year* Print a 12-month calendar for the specified *year* or a single *month*. *month* a digit (1-12) specifying the month (e.g., *cal 12 1984*). *year* a digit (1-9999) specifying the year (e.g., *cal 1984*).
calendar	**calendar** [*options*] Read the **calendar** file, located in your login directory, and send all lines (via mail) that contain the current date. *options* **-** invoke calendar for all users.
cat	**cat** [*options*] [*files*] Read and print one or more *files*. Several files may be combined and directed to another file with the > operator (*e.g., cat ch1 ch2 ch3 > ch1-3*). If no files are specified, read from standard input; end with ^D.

options

-e	display non-printing characters including a $ prior to each new-line. To be used with the -v option.	**cat**
		continued

-n precede every line with a line number.

-b omit line numbers from blank lines. To be used with the **-n** option.

-s replace multiple adjacent blank lines with a single blank line.

-t display non-printing characters including a ˆI in place of tabs. To be used with the **-v** option.

-v display non-printing characters.

---

cb [*files*]

C program "beautifier" that formats *files* using proper C programming structure.

cb

---

cc [*options*] *files*

cc

Compile one or more C (*file*.c) or assembler (*file*.s) source files. Output is placed in **a.out** by default.

options

-B *string*
find substitute compiler passes in files named *string* with suffixes *cpp*, *ccom*, and *c2*.

-c suppress the loading phase.

-C do not strip comments.

-D *name*[*=def*]
define *name* as *def* (default is 1).

-E run only the macro preprocessor.

-f *option*
use the floating-point interpreter *option*. (*system dependent*)

-g[o] generate a symbol table needed for the debugger **dbx**, or for **sdb** if the **o** flag is used.

-I *dir* add directory *dir* to #include file search path.

☞

cc
continued
	-L *dir* add *dir* to library archive search path.
	-M run only the macro preprocessor, generating Makefile dependencies to standard output.
	-o *file* put output in *file*.
	-O invoke an object code optimizer.
	-p[g] count the times each routine is called. With the **g** flag, keep more extensive statistics and produce the file **gmon.out** at normal termination.
	-R make initialized variables read-only and shared.
	-t[p012]
	     use the specified compiler options.
	-U *name*
	     remove definition of *name*.
	-w suppress warning messages.
	There may be other machine-specific options.

ccat	**ccat** *file* Display a compacted *file* on standard output. See **compact**.
cd	**cd** [*directory*] Change the current working directory to *directory*. If *directory* not specified, change to user's home directory.

cdc *scs*	**cdc** [*options*] *files*
	
	Change the delta comments for one or more SCCS *files*. See also **sccs**; see Section 9 for more information on SCCS.
	
	options
	  -m [*list*]
	     add the *list* of modification request numbers.
	  -r *sid* SCCS delta id version number.
	  -y [*string*]
	     replace comment with *string*.

checkeq *files*

Check the **eqn** constructs in *files*.

checkeq

---

checknr [*options*] *files*

Check **nroff** or **troff** *files* for errors.

options

    -a.*x1.y1.x2.y2 ... xn.yn*
        add additional pairs of macros; for example
        -a.CS.CE
    -c.*x1.y1.x2.y2 .... xn.yn*
        define commands that would otherwise
        generate warning messages.
    -f   ignore \f font changes.
    -s   ignore \s size changes.

checknr

---

chgrp *newgroup files*

Change the ownership of one or more *files* to *new-group*. *newgroup* is either a group id number or a group name located in **/etc/group**.

chgrp

---

chmod [*options*] *permission files*

Change the access mode of one or more *files*. Only the owner of a file or a superuser may change its mode.

options

    -R   recursively descend directory arguments
           while setting modes.
    -f   suppress message upon failure to change
          the mode on a file.

Create *permission* by concatenating members of *who*, *opcode*, and *mode*.

who

    u   user.
    g   group.
    o   other.
    a   all.

chmod

chmod
continued

opcode

    +   add permission.
    -   remove permission.
    =   assign permission.

mode

    r   read.
    w   write.
    x   execute.
    s   set user (or group) id.
    t   save text (sticky) mode.
    u   user's present permission.
    g   group's present permission.
    o   other's present permission.

For example, **chmod u+x** *file* will add execute-by-user permission to *file*.

Alternatively, specify permissions by a 3-digit sequence. The first digit designates owner permission; the second, group permission; and the third, others permission. Digits are calculated as a compilation of the following values:

    4 read
    2 write
    1 execute

For example, **chmod 751** *file* makes *file* read-write-execute by owner, read-execute by group, and execute-only for others.

chown

chown *newowner files*

Change the ownership of one or more *files* to *newowner*. *newowner* is either a user id number or a login name located in **/etc/passwd**.

chsh

chsh *user* [*shell*]

Change *user*'s login shell to *shell*. Like **passwd**, this command modifies the **/etc/passwd** file and thus takes effect when the user next logs in.

clear	**clear**

Clear the terminal display.

cmp [*options*] *file1 file2*	**cmp**

Compare *file1* with *file2* and print the differing byte
and line numbers.

options

   -l   print byte number and differing bytes.
   -s   print only the return codes:
               0 = files are identical.
               1 = files are different.
               2 = files are inaccessible.

col [*options*]	**col**

Perform line overlays as specified by reverse line-
feeds and by forward and reverse half-line feeds. Useful for filtering output produced by the **.rt** command of
nroff or by **tbl**.

options

   -b   ignore backspace characters.
   -f   perform forward half-line feeds.
   -h   convert spaces to tabs.

colcrt [*options*] [*files*]	**colcrt**

Provide virtual half-line and reverse line feeds on the
specified *files* for terminals without this capability.
This command is used for previewing **nroff** output.

options

   -   suppress underlining.
   -2   double space the output.

colrm [*startcol* [*endcol*]]	**colrm**

Remove columns in each line for a named file. A
range of columns is specified by *startcol* and *endcol*.

comb

comb [*options*] *files*

Combine SCCS deltas of the named *files*. See also sccs; for more information on SCCS, see Section 9.

options

    -c *list* preserve the deltas in *list*. *list* syntax can be found in **get** description.

    -o   access "as created" file instead of most recent.

    -p *sid* oldest delta version number to be preserved.

    -s   generate a shell file which prints space savings data.

comm

comm [*options*] *file1 file2*

Compare lines common to the sorted files *file1* and *file2*. Three-column output is produced with each column containing either lines only in *file1*, lines only in *file2*, or lines in both *files*.

options

    -   read the standard input.

    -1   suppress printing of column 1.

    -2   suppress printing of column 2.

    -3   suppress printing of column 3.

    -12 print only the lines common to *file1* and *file2*.

    -23 print only the lines in *file1* but not *file2*.

compact

compact [*files*]

Compact one or more files using Huffman coding and place the result in *file*.C. To restore and read compressed files, use **uncompact** or **ccat**. See also **compress** and **pack**.

compress

compress [*options*] [*files*]

Reduce the size of one or more files using adaptive Lempel-Ziv coding and place the file in *file*.Z. Restore with **uncompress** or **zcat**.

options

compress
continued

-f   compress unconditionally, i.e. do not prompt before overwriting files.

-v   print the resulting percentage of reduction for each file.

-c   write to the standard output: do not change files.

-b*n*   limit the number of bits in coding to *n* (default = 16).

---

cp *file1 file2*
cp [-f] *files directory*

cp

Copy *file1* to *file2*, or copy one or more files to specified directory under same name. If destination file already exists, it will be overwritten.

options

-i   prompt for permission to overwrite.

-p   preserve in copies the modification times and modes of the source files.

-r   if the destination is a directory, copy all source files and directories to the destination.

---

cpio *options flags*

cpio

Copy file archives in or out from tape or disk. Each of the three options has different flags, as follows:

cpio -o [aBcv]
Copy out a list of files whose names are given on the standard input.

cpio -i [bBcdmrdsStuv6] [*patterns*]
Copy in files whose names match selected *patterns* in the style of **sh** and **csh**. (Patterns should be quoted or escaped so they are interpreted by **cpio**, not the shell.)

cpio -p [adlmruv] *directory*
Copy files out and in. Destination pathnames are interpreted relative to the named *directory*.

flags

a   reset access times of input files.

cpio *continued*	**s**	swap bytes, headers only.
	t	print a table of contents for the input.
	u	copy unconditionally.
	v	print a list of filenames.
	6	UNIX sixth edition format (used only with -i).

patterns

Names of files to select, in shell notation. (Default is *, all files. Patterns should be quoted or escaped so they are interpreted by **cpio**, not the shell.)

directories

Destination pathnames.

---

cpp

cpp [*options*] [*ifile*] [*ofile*]

Run the C preprocessor on the input *ifile* and place the output in *ofile*.

options

    -R   permit recursive macros.

    -U *name*

          undefine the definition for *name*.

control directives

#define, #else, #endif, #ifndef, #if, #ifdef, #include, #line, #undef

---

crypt

crypt [*password*] < *file* > *encryptedfile*

Encrypt a *file* to prevent unauthorized access. The same *password* is used to encrypt a file or decrypt an encrypted file. If no password is specified, **crypt** prompts for one.

---

csh

csh [*options*] [*arguments*]

C shell command interpreter.

options

    -c   read commands from the specified *argument*.

    -e   exit if any invoked command terminates abnormally.

-f	do not read or execute commands from .cshrc.	**csh** *continued*

-f do not read or execute commands from .cshrc.
-i interactive shell.
-n parse commands but do not execute.
-s take command input from standard input.
-t read and execute a single line of input.
-v echo command input after history substitution.
-V set verbose variable before .cshrc is executed.
-x set echo variable, commands are echoed immediately before execution.
-X set echo variable before .cshrc is executed.

---

ctags [*options*] *files*   **ctags**

Create a file containing the location of specified functions from the named C, Pascal, FORTRAN, YACC, lex, or lisp source *files*.

options

-a append output to tags file.
-B use backward search.
-F use forward search.
-t use tags for typedefs.
-u delete file references and append new values.
-v produce an index of the form in **vgrind** on the standard output.
-w suppress warning messages.
-x produce a list of function names, line numbers, filenames, and text.
-f *tagsfile*
    place tags description in *tagsfile* (default = tags).

---

date [*options*] [*yymmddhhmm* [*.ss*]]   **date**

Display the current date and time. A superuser may set the date and time in *yymmddhhmm.ss* format.

options

-n set time only on local machine if *timed* is running in a local area network.

☞

date *continued*	**-u** use the Greenwich Mean Time. [yy] last two digits of the year (e.g., *84*). *mm* month number (e.g., *12*). *dd* day number (e.g., *25*). *hhmm* hour and minute (24-hour clock). *.ss* optional seconds

---

dbx

dbx *[options]* *[objfile [corefile]]*

Source code debugger for the C, Pascal, and FORTRAN languages. *objfile* contains an executable program and *corefile* contains the core image produced when *objfile* is executed. **a.out** is the default *objfile*. **core** is the default *corefile*. See Section 8 for more information on **dbx**.

options

    -i   force standard input terminal or terminal emulator type function.

    -I*dir* add *dir* to the directory search path.

    -k   use Kernel debug mode.

    -r   execute *objfile* without waiting.

    -c*file* execute **dbx** commands from *file* before reading standard input.

---

dc

dc *[file]*

An interactive desk calculator program that performs precision integer arithmetic (input may be taken from a *file*). The input and output number base, as well as the number of fractional digits, can be specified by the user.

---

dd

dd *[options]*

Make a copy of an input file with the specified conversions and send the results to the output file, or standard output if **of** is not specified.

options

    bs=*n* set input and output block size to *n* bytes.

    cbs=*n* set conversion buffer size to *n*.

conv=	=ascii	EBCDIC to ASCII.
	=block	variable to fixed length records.
	=ebcdic	ASCII to EBCDIC.
	=ibm	ASCII to EBCDIC with IBM conventions.
	=lcase	upper case to lower case.
	=noerror	continue when an error occurs.
	=swab	swap all pairs of bytes.
	=sync	pad input records to ibs.
	=ucase	lower case to upper case.
	=unblock	fixed records become variable length.
	=...,...	more than one conversion, comma-separated.

dd
continued

count=*n*
  copy only *n* input records.
files=*n*
  skip *n* input files.
ibs=*n* set input block size to *n* bytes (default is 512).
if=*file* input filename is *file* (default is standard input).
obs=*n* set output block size to *n* bytes (default is 512).
of=*file*
  output to *file* (default is standard output).
seek=*n*
  seek *n* records from start of output file.
skip=*n*
  skip *n* input records.

The output is written as if filtered through "od -c". It is blocked by "input record". If *tape* is specified also, that information will precede each block dumped. This may be useful when examining unknown tapes.

delta [*options*] *files*

delta

Incorporate changes to one or more SCCS *files*. See also sccs; see Section 9 for more information on SCCS.

delta
continued
	options
	    -g*list* ignore deltas in *list*.
	    -m[*list*]
	            list of modification request numbers.
	    -n save changes file *file.g*.
	    -p print delta references.
	    -r*sid* delta version number.
	    -s suppress printing of new SCCS id.
	    -y[*string*]
	            insert *string* as a comment.

deroff	**deroff** [*options*] [*files*] Ignore all **nroff, troff, tbl,** and **eqn** requests from the named *files*. *options* **-w** output a word list, one word per line.

des	**des** [*options*] [*ifile* [*ofile*]]
	
	Encrypt or decrypt *ifile* and place output in *ofile*. The standard input and output are the default files.
	options
	    -b use eight byte encryption mode.
	    -d decrypt the *ifile*.
	    -e encrypt the *ifile*.
	    -f suppress warning messages.
	    -k*key* use the encryption *key*.
	    -s select software implementation.

df	**df** [*options*] [*filesystems*] [*files*] Report the number of free blocks and i-nodes available for the named *filesystems*, or on the filesystem on which *files* reside. If neither *filesystem* nor *files* is specified, display values for all mounted filesystems. *options* **-i** report the number of inodes used.

diction [*options*] *files*   **diction**

Print grammatically incorrect sentences contained in
one or more *files*. See also **explain**.

options

-**f** *file*   search *file* for the undesirable words and
            phrases.

-**ml**   ignore lists of non-sentences.

-**mm**   use -**mm** macro package rather than **ms**.

-**n**   do not read default pattern file.

---

diff [*options*] *file1 file2*   **diff**
diff [*diroptions*] *dir1 dir2*

Report the lines that differ between *file1* and *file2*, or if
diroptions are specified, report the files that differ
between *directory1* and *directory2*.

options

-**b**   ignore blank spaces and tabs.

-**c***n*   produce *n* lines of context (default is 3).

-**e**   produce a file of edit commands to recreate
         file2 from *file1* using **ed**.

-**f**   recreate *file1* from *file2* but not with **ed**.

-**h**   perform the comparison quickly.

-**n**   produce a file of edit commands to recreate
         file1 from *file2*, and counting changed
         lines.

-**D***string*
         create a merged version of *file1* and *file2*
         on standard output.

-**w**   ignore all whitespace (blanks and tabs).

-**i**   ignore upper and lower case distinction.

-**t**   expand tabs on output (useful with -**c**).

The above options are mutually exclusive, except for
-**b**, -**w**, -**i**, and -**t**.

diroptions

-**l**   long output format.

-**r**   recursive **diff** for common subdirectories.

-**s**   report files that are identical.

-**S***file*   begin directory comparison with *file*.

diff3	**diff3** [*options*] *file1 file2 file3*
	Compare three files and report the differences with the following codes:

diff3 [*options*] *file1 file2 file3*

Compare three files and report the differences with the following codes:

    ==   all three files differ.
    ==1   *file1* is different.
    ==2   *file2* is different.
    ==3   *file3* is different.

options

    -e   create an editor script to incorporate into *file1* all changes between *file2* and *file3*.
    -E   same as **-e**, but treat overlapping changes differently.
    -x   create an editor script to incorporate into *file1* all differences between all three files.
    -X   same as **-x**, but treat overlapping changes differently.
    -3   create an editor script to incorporate into *file1* all differences between *file1* and *file3*.

disable

disable [*options*] *name*

Deactivate the printer *name*.

options

    -c   cancel all active print jobs.
    -r"*reason***"**
        associate *reason* with this deactivation.

du

du [*options*] [*directories*]

Print the number of blocks used by each subdirectory in named directory or directories. The current directory is the default.

options

    -a   produce an entry for each file in each named directory.
    -s *dir*   print only the grand total for each named directory *dir*.

echo [*options*] [*string*]   **echo**

Copy *string* to the standard output. If *string* not specified, echo a newline. See Section 2 for more information on **echo**.

options

  -n   don't add a newline to *string*.

---

ed [*options*] [*file*]   **ed**

The standard text editor. If the named *file* does not exist, **ed** will create it; otherwise the existing named *file* will be opened for editing.

options

  -   suppress character counts, diagnostics, and ! prompt.
  -p   user defined prompt string.
  -x   read an encrypted file.

---

edit [*file*]   **edit**

A line-oriented text editor.

---

efl [*options*] [*files*]   **efl**

Convert a file from EFL (Extended FORTRAN Language) to FORTRAN. Used as a preprocessor for **f77**.

options

  -w   suppress warning messages.
  -C   copy comments through to the FORTRAN output (default).
  -#   do not copy comments through.

---

egrep [*options*] [*regexp*] [*files*]   **egrep**

Search one or more *files* for lines that match a full regular expression *regexp*. Regular expressions are listed in Section 3. See also **grep** and **fgrep**.

☞

egrep *continued*	*options*
	-b precede each line with block number.
	-c print only count of matched lines.
	-e *expr*
	use this option if *expr* contains a leading hyphen.
	-f *file* take expression from *file*.
	-l list only file names.
	-n precede each line with line number.
	-s silent mode: print only error messages.
	-v print all non-matching lines.

---

enroll

enroll

Enter the protected mail system. **enroll** prompts for a password. See also **xsend** and **xget**.

---

eqn *troff*

eqn [*options*] [*files*]

Numerical equation preprocessor for **troff**. See Section 7 for more information on **eqn**. Use **neqn** with **nroff**.

options

    -dxy use x and y as start and stop delimiters.
    -fn change to font n.
    -pn reduce the superscript size by n points.
    -sn reduce the point size by n points.

---

error

error [*options*] [*file*]

Analyze compiler error messages from *file* or from standard input, and change the source file to reflect the error.

options

    -I*ignorefile*
        ignore functions listed in *ignorefile*.
    -n   write to standard output, not to the source file.
    -q   ask whether a file should be touched.
    -s   report statistics.

-t *suffixl*	**error**
suffixl is the list of valid file suffixes which **error** operate on.	*continued*
-v enter *vi* after **error** completes.	

---

ex [*options*] *files*   **ex**

A line-oriented text editor — a superset of **ed** and the root of **vi**. See Section 4 for more information on **ex**.

options

-     suppress all warning, interactive, and error messages.
- **-l**   edit a LISP file.
- **-r**   recover a file(s).
- **-R**   open a file in read only mode.
- **-t** *tag* begin editing at *tag* location.
- **-v**   invoke **vi**.
- **-x**   provide key to decrypt *file*.
- **+** *command*
      execute *command* when invoking **ex**.

---

expand [*options*] [*files*]   **expand**

Convert all tab characters to blank spaces in the named *files*. See also **unexpand**.

options

- **-n**   set tab stops *n* spaces apart (default is 8).
- **-n1,n2,n3 ...**
      set tab stops at *n1,n2,n3,...* (e.g., *-4,8,12*).

---

explain   **explain**

An interactive thesaurus for phrases found by **diction**.

---

expr *arguments*   **expr**

Evaluate the named *arguments* as expressions and print the result. Expression elements and operators must be separated by spaces.

☞

expr *continued*	*arguments*

arguments

    expr1 | expr2
        True if either expression *expr1* or *expr2* is
        true.

    expr1 & expr2
        True if expression *expr1* or *expr2* are both
        true.

    expr1 {op} expr2
        yield 1 if the indicated comparison is true,
        0 if false. *op* is one of the following: =, , =,
        , =, !=.

    expr1 + expr2
        add the expressions.

    expr1 - expr2
        subtract the expressions.

    *expr1 * expr2*
        multiply the expressions.

    expr1 / expr2
        divide the expressions.

    expr1 % expr2
        take the remainder after division of the
        arguments.

    expr1 : expr2
        compare *expr1* with *expr2*.
        expr2 must be regular.

    (expr) evaluate expressions enclosed in parenthe-
        ses first. (Expressions are normally
        evaluated left to right.)

The characters &, |, and * must be escaped (preceded
with \).

---

eyacc	**eyacc** [*options*] [*grammar*]

Efficient version of **yacc**. See also **yacc**.

options

Options are identical to those of **yacc**.

---

f77	**f77** [*options*] *files*

The UNIX FORTRAN 77 compiler.

options

-c   suppress compilation loading and produce
        .o files.
-C   check that subscripts are within declared
        boundaries.
-d   debug the compiler.
-D *name*[=*def*]
        define *name* as *def* (default is 1).
-f *option*
        use the floating point processor *option*.
-F   invoke EFL and RATFOR preprocessor and
        place the result in *file*.**f**.
-g   create additional symbol table information.
-i2   make the default integer constants and
        variables short.
-I *dir*   additional directory for include files.
-m   invoke **m4** preprocessor to RATFOR or EFL
        file.
-N *flag*
        establish the maximum size of various
        dynamically allocated compiler internal
        data structures.
        flag is one of:
        c - number of looping structures
        n - number of identifiers
        q - number of equivalences
        s - number of statement numbers
        x - number of external names
-o *file*   place output in *file* (default is **a.out**).
-O   invoke object code optimizer.
-onetrip, -1
        compile DO loops.
-p   set up object files for profiling.
-pg   set up object files for extensive profiling.
-q   suppress printing of file and program unit
        names while compiling.
-r8   treat floating point constructs as double
        precision and complex quantities as double
        complex.
-R *string*
        use *string* as RATFOR option.
-S   produce assembler .**s** files.
-u   variable type undefined.

f77 *continued*	**-U** do not convert upper case letters to lower case. **-v** print compilation progress report. **-w** suppress warning messages.
false	**false** Return unsuccessful exit status. See also **true**.

fed *H-P 2648*	**fed** [*options*] *file*
	
	Font file editor used on Hewlett-Packard 2648 graphics terminal. Many commands are available in **fed**. See also **vfont**, **vtroff**, and **vwidth**.
	options
	    -i inverse video mode, which provides a setting similar to the hardcopy output of the plotter.
	    -q quiet mode, which suppresses all graphic output and speeds up **fed**.

fgrep	**fgrep** [*options*] [*pattern*] [*files*]
	
	Search one or more *files* for lines that match a fixed-string *pattern*. **fgrep** does not support regular expressions. See also **egrep** and **grep**.
	options
	    -b precede each line with block number.
	    -c print only count of matched lines.
	    -e*pattern*
	        this option is for *pattern* which begin with "-".
	    -f*file* take pattern from *file*.
	    -i ignore upper and lower case distinction.
	    -l list only filenames.
	    -n precede each line with line number.
	    -s silent mode: print only error messages.
	    -v print only non-matching lines.
	    -x print only lines that match exactly.

file *files*   **file**

Classify the named *files*, according to the type of data
they contain. file checks the magic file (usually
/etc/magic) to identify files containing a numeric or
string constant indicating its type.

find *pathnames condition(s)*   **find**

Search one or more *pathnames* for files that meet the
specified *condition*. At least one *pathname* and one
condition must be specified. Conditions may be
grouped using escaped parentheses (\(and \)), negated
with !, or given as alternatives by separating them with
-o. If you want the results of the search to be
displayed, be sure to use the **-print** option.

condition

-name *name*

> only files which match the specified name.
> Shell metacharacters may be used, but
> should be escaped or quoted.

-perm *onum*

> only files with file permission flags exactly
> matching the octal number *onum*.

-type *c*

> only files whose type is *c*. *c* may be **b**
> (block special file), **c** (character special
> file), **d** (directory), **p** (fifo or named pipe),
> or **f** (plain file).

-links *n*

> only files with *n* links.

-user *uname*

> only files belonging to the user *uname*.
> *uname* may be a user name or a *uid* num-
> ber.

-group *gname*

> only files belonging to the group *gname*.
> *gname* may be a user name or a *gid* num-
> ber.

-size *n*[c]

> only files which are *n* blocks long, or if **c** is
> specified, *n* characters long.

-inum *n*

> only files with i-node number *n*.

☞

find
continued

-atime [+,-]*n*
> only files that were last accessed more than (+*n*), less than (-*n*), or exactly *n* days.

-mtime [+,-]*n*
> only files that were last modified more than (+*n*), less than (-*n*), or exactly *n* days.

-exec *cmd* {}\;
> only files that return a zero value as exit status when *cmd* is executed. Within the command, the argument {} is replaced with the current pathname. The entire sequence must be followed with an escaped semicolon (\;).

-ok *cmd* {}\;
> same as -exec, except that user is prompted before executing.

-print print the pathname of each selected file.

-ls print current path with associated statistics.

-newer *file*
> only files that have been modified more recently than *file*.

-xdev do not traverse into file system different from one on which current pathname resides.

finger

finger [*options*] *user*

Print an expanded list of information about each UNIX *user*, using **.plan** and **.project** files in the user's home directory.

options

-l force the long output format.

-m match arguments by user name only.

-p suppress printing of the **.plan** files.

-s force the short output format.

fmt

fmt [*files*]

Format simple text *files* (e.g., mail messages), into lines approximately 72-characters long..

fold [*options*] [*files*]   **fold**

Break the lines of the named *files* so that they are no
wider than the specified width. **fold** will break lines
exactly at the specified width, even in the middle of a
word.

options

   -n   set width to *n* (default is 80).

---

fp   **fp**

Functional programming language compiler and interpreter. help summarizes all user commands.

---

fpr   *Fortran*   **fpr**

FORTRAN printer filter. Files are converted from FOR-
TRAN output format so that they print correctly with
lpr.

---

from [*options*] [*user*]   **from**

Print out mail headers in *user*'s mailbox file to determine from whom the mail was sent. Default is own
mailbox file.

options

   -ssender
       print only headers from *sender*.

---

fsplit [*options*] *files*   *Fortran*   **fsplit**

Split a FORTRAN file into program segments if possible.

options

   -esegment
       only split *segment* into a new file. This
       option can be used several times on a
       single command line.

---

ftp

ftp [*options*] [*hostname*]

Transfer files to and from remote network site *hostname*. **ftp** prompts the user for a command. Type **help** to see a list of known commands.

options

-d	enable debugging.
-g	disable file name globbing.
-i	turn off interactive prompting.
-n	no auto-login upon initial connection.
-v	verbose on. Show all responses from the remote server.

gcore

gcore *process id* . . .

Create ("get") a core image of each running process. The core image can be used with **adb** or **dbx**.

get *sccs*

get [*options*] *files*

Retrieve a particular version of an SCCS *file* and print its version number and total number of lines. For more information on SCCS, see Section 9.

options

-a*n*	retrieve delta sequence number *n*.
-b	create new branch.
-c*date*	ignore changes made after *date* (format *yy*[*mm*[*dd*[*hh*[*mm*[*ss*]]]]]).
-e	retrieve for editing.
-g	suppress version retrieval.
-i*list*	include a *list* of changes.
-k	do not replace id keywords.
-l[**p**]*file*	write delta summary to *file*. **-lp** displays a summary.
-m	precede each line with sid version number.
-n	precede each line with %M% keyword.
-p	write retrieved text to standard output.
-r*sid*	retrieve version number *sid*.
-s	suppress normal output.
-t	retrieve latest version of a release.

gprof [*options*] [*objfile* [*pfile*]]   **gprof**

Display call graph profile data of C, Pascal, or f77 programs. Programs compiled with the **-pg** option of **cc**, **pc**, and **f77** produce a call graph profile file *pfile*, whose default name is **gmon.out**. The specified object file *objfile* (**a.out** by default) contains a symbol table which is read and correlated with *pfile*.

options

-a   suppress printing of statically declared functions.

-b   suppress printing of a description of each field in the profile.

-c   find the static call graph of the program. Call counts of 0 indicate static-only parents or children.

-e *name*
     suppress printing of the graph profile entry for the routine *name*. This option may be repeated.

-E *name*
     like -e above, but also excludes the time spent in *name* from the time computations.

-f *name*
     print the graph profile entry of only the routine *name*. This option may be repeated.

-F *name*
     like -f above, but also uses only the times of the printed routines in time computations. This option overrides the -E option.

-s   sum the information in all specified profile files and send it to a profile file called **gmon.sum**.

-z   display routines which have zero usage. Use with the -c option to discover which routines were never called.

graph [*options*]   **graph**

Draw a graph, using pairs of numbers taken from standard input as *x-y* coordinates. The graph may be printed using **plot**. See also **spline**.

☞

graph
continued

options

  -a *spacing* [*start*]

      provide abscissas with *spacing* (default 1) and starting point *start* (default 0).

  -b   break after each input.

  -c *string*

      label each point with *string*.

  -g *n*   grid style: 0=no grid, 1=tick grid, 2=full grid.

  -h *n*   space *n* height.

  -l *label*

      use *label* for the graph.

  -m *n*   connecting lines style: 0=disconnected, 1=connected.

  -r *n*   move fraction *n* right before plotting.

  -s   save screen.

  -t   transpose axes.

  -u *n*   move fraction *n* up before plotting.

  -w *n*   space *n* height.

  -x [l] *lower upper spacing*

      manual x-axis layout. The optional l gives a logarithmic axis.

  -y [l] *lower upper spacing*

      manual y-axis layout. The optional l gives a logarithmic axis.

grep

grep [*options*] *regexp* [*files*]

Search one or more *files* for a regular expression *regexp*. Regular expressions are described in Section 3. See also **egrep** and **fgrep**.

options

  -b   precede each line block number.

  -c   print only a count of matched lines.

  -e *expr*

      used to specify an *expr* with a leading hyphen.

  -f *file* take regular expression from *file*.

  -h   do not print filenames.

  -i   ignore upper/lower case distinctions.

  -l   print only the names of files containing matching lines.

-n precede each line with line number. **-s** suppress error messages. **-v** print only non-matching lines. **-w** search for the expression as it were a word.	**grep** *continued*
groups [*user*] Display your group, or that of specified *user*.	**groups**
head [*options*] [*files*] Print the first few lines of one or more *files*. *options* **-n** print the first *n* lines (default is 10).	**head**
help [*command*] [*error*] Give an explanation of a *command* or an *error* message number.	**help**
hostid [*id*] Report the host system's identification number, or set it to be *id* (super-user only).	**hostid**
hostname [*newname*] Report the host system's name, or set it to be *newname* (super-user only).	**hostname**

indent [*ifile* [*ofile*]] [*options*]
 	
 Format *ifile* in C program structure. The output is placed in *ofile* or, if *ofile* is unspecified, output is placed in *ifile* and *ifile* is moved to *ifile*.**BAK**.
 options
     -bad force a blank line after every block of declarations. Turn off with **-nbad** (default).
     -bap force a blank line after every procedure body. Turn off with **-nbap** (default).
 	
 ☞
	indent

indent
continued

-bbb	force a blank line before every block comment. Turn off with **-nbbb** (default).
-bc	add a newline after each comma in a declaration (the default). Turn off with **-nbc** (default).
-bl	line up complex statements with left curly brace at the end of initial line. Place left curly brace on separate line with **-br** (default).
-c*n*	start comment in column *n* (default is 33).
-cd*n*	start declaration comments in column *n* (default is same as other comments).
-cdb	place comment delimiters on separate lines (default). Turn off with **-ncdb**.
-ce	force "else" to be adjacent to preceding ")". Turn off with **-nce** (default).
-ci*n*	set the continuation indent to *n* (default = 8).
-cli*n*	indent case labels *n* tab stops to the right of continuing **switch** statement. *n* may be in decimal. Default is 0.
-d*n*	place comments *n* indent levels left of the code (default lines up with code).
-di*n*	indent *n* character positions from a declaration keyword to the following identifier.
-dj	left justify declarations. Turn off with **-ndj** (default), which indents declarations the same amount as code.
-ei	indent **ifs** following **elses** the same as preceding **if** statement (default). Turn off with **-nei**.
-fc1	format comments starting in column 1 (default). To allow manual formatting, turn off with **-nfc1**.
-i*n*	change the indentation level to *n* (default is 4).
-ip	indent parameter declarations from left margin (default). Turn off with **-nip**.
-l*n*	set line length to *n* (default is 78).
-lp	line up code surrounded by parentheses in continuation lines under the left paren (default). Turn off with **-nlp**.
-npro	ignore profile files *./.indent.pro* and *~/.indent.pro*.

-pcs	insert a space between left paren and name in procedure calls. Turn off with **-npcs** (default).	**indent** *continued*

-ps   surround "->" by spaces. Turn off with **-nps** (default).

-ps1   place names of procedures being defined in column 1 with types left on previous lines (default). Turn off with **-nps1**.

-sc   place asterisks at the left edge of comments (default). Turn off with **-nsc**.

-sob   force indent to swallow blank lines. Turn off with **-nsob** (default).

-st   take input from **stdin** and place output in **stdout**.

-T *name*
    add *name* to list of type keywords.

-troff format the program for processing by **troff**.

-v   report when one line of input is split. Turn off with **-nv** (default).

---

indxbib *database* . . .   *fil*   **indxbib**

Make an inverted index for *database*. See also **refer** and **lookbib**.

---

install [*options*] *file destination*   **install**

Move the binary *file* to the *destination* file or directory.
    -c   copy *file* rather than move it.
    -g *group*
        assign the file *dest* to *group*.
    -m *mode*
        assign *mode* to the file *dest*.
    -o *owner*
        assign *owner* to the file *dest*.
    -s   strip *file* after it is copied.

---

iostat [*drives*] [*interval* [*count*]]   **iostat**

Report I/O statistics iteratively, every *interval* seconds. Force specific drives to be displayed with *drives*; specify the number of reports with *count*. The first interval is always the time since the last reboot.

join

join [*options*] *file1 file2*

Join the common lines of sorted *file1* and sorted *file2*. The output contains the common field and the remainder of each line from *file1* and *file2*.

options

-a*n* list unpairable lines in file *n* (*n* is 1 or 2).

-e *string*
  replace empty output fields with *string*.

-j*n m* join on the *m*th field of file *n* (where *n* is 1 or 2). If *n* is omitted, use the *m*th field in each file.

-o *list* output line contains the fields specified in *list*; each element has the form *n.m* (*n* is file number, and *m* is field number).

-t*c* use *c* as field separator (default is a tab).

jove

jove [*options*] [*files*]

EMACS-compatible text editor. For a list of commands, type **<ESC>X?RETURN**

options

-d*dir* specify name of current directory.

-w divide window into two.

-t*tag* run **find-tag** on *tag*.

+n*file* position point on *n*th line instead of first.

-p*file* parse error messages found in *file*.

kill

kill [*-signal*] *pid*

Terminate a process. You must be either the owner of the process or a superuser.

-l list signal names.

-signal
  the signal number or name. With a signal number of 9, the kill is absolute.

pid the process id number (obtained from **ps**). Using the C Shell, you can kill using job specifiers as well as *pids*.

last [*options*] [*users*] [*ttys*]   **last**

List a history of login sessions associated with *users*
or *ttys*, with the most recent session first. With no
arguments, list all login sessions. The listing includes
the user name, tty#, date, and the duration of the session.

options

    -ffile   search *file* for login information (the
               default is **/usr/adm/wtmp**).
    -n   limit the output to *n* lines.

---

lastcomm [*commands*] [*users*] [*ttys*]   **lastcomm**

List the administrative information stored about the
user, tty#, date, and other system information on previously issued commands. With no arguments, list
information about all commands in record. By default,
lastcomm lists all commands recorded in
/usr/lib/acct. You can also request information for
particular *commands*, *users*, or *ttys*.

---

ld [*options*] *objfiles*   **ld**

Combine several *objfiles*, in the specified order, into a
single object module (**a.out**).

options

    -A   incremental loading.
    -d   force the definition of common storage.
    -D *hex* pad the data with zeros until it is *hex* bytes
           long.
    -e *name*
           name of entry point (default is location 0).
    -l*x*   search the library **/lib/lib***x***.a** or
           /usr/lib/lib*x***.a** (the placement of this option
           is significant).
    -L *dir* add *dir* to the list of directories in which to
           search for libraries.
    -M   produce a primitive load map.
    -n   create output file as read-only.
    -N   do not make text portion read-only or shar-
           able.

☞

ld *continued*	**-o** *file*	send the output to *file* (default is **a.out**).
	-r	allow output to be subject to another **ld**.
	-s	remove symbol table and relocation bits.
	-S	remove all symbols except locals and globals.
	-t	print the name of each file as it is processed.
	-T *n*	set text segment origin at hexadecimal number *n* (default is 0).
	-u *sym*	enter *sym* in symbol table.
	-x	enter only external symbols in output.
	-X	save all local symbols except those beginning with "L."
	-y *sym*	indicate each file in which *sym* appears, its type and whether the file defines or references it.
	-z	arrange the file to be loaded on demand from the resulting executable file.

---

learn

learn [*options*] [*subject* [*lesson*]]

A program which provides computer-aided mini-courses. Type **learn** to see instructions on how to use the program. Type **bye** to exit **learn**.

options

-*dir* exercise a script in a non-standard place.
-*dirname*
      allow the user to exercise a script in a non-standard place.

subject

The subjects currently handled are:

files	morefiles
editor	macros
vi	eqn
C	

Each subject is covered in one or more *lessons*.

---

leave

leave [[+] *time*]

Remind you when it's time to leave. Set off an alarm five minutes and one minute before the specified time, at the specified time, and every minute thereafter. *time*

---

is in the form *hhmm* for the actual time or *+hhmm*, for hours and minutes from the current time.

leave
continued

---

lex [*options*] [*files*]

lex

Generate lexical analysis programs from regular expressions and C program actions.

options

- **-f**   use the faster compilation.
- **-n**   do not print statistical summary.
- **-t**   write lex program to standard output instead of **lex.yy.c**.
- **-v**   print summary of machine-generated statistics.

---

lint [*options*] *files*

lint

Detect bugs, portability problems, and other possible errors in the specified C programs. By default, function definitions are defined in the **llib-lc.ln** library.

options

- **-a**   ignore long values assigned to variables that are not long.
- **-b**   ignore break statements that cannot be reached.
- **-c**   report casts that are not portable.
- **-C***name*
   create a *lint* library **llib-l***name***.ln**.
- **-D**   same as **-D** of **cc**.
- **-h**   apply tests for bugs, style, and extraneous information.
- **-I**   same as **-I** of **cc**
- **-l***lib*   use *lib* from **/usr/lib/lint**.
- **-n**   do not check for compatibility.
- **-p**   check portability to IBM and GCOS dialects of C.
- **-u**   ignore undefined functions and variables.
- **-U***name*
   remove an initial definition of *name*.
- **-v**   ignore unused arguments within functions.
- **-x**   ignore unused variables referred to by external declarations.

☞

---

lint *continued*	**-z** do not issue undefined structure messages.
lisp	**lisp**
	A list interpreter for a dialect called FRANZ LISP. See LISP manuals for available functions.
listrefs *lil*	**listrefs** [*options*]
	Format a reference database file.
	options
	Options are the same as for **bib**.
liszt	**liszt** [*options*] [*pfile*]
	FRANZ LISP compiler. The name of program file *pfile* ends in **.l**; the returned object file name ends in **.o**.
	options

      -C   put comments in the assembler output of the compiler.

      -e *form*
          evaluate *form* before compilation.

      -m   compile a MACLISP file, making the program file compatible with MACLISP syntax.

      -o *objfile*
          put the object code in *objfile* rather than the default **.o** file.

      -p   place profiling code at the beginning of each non-local function.

      -q   print warning and error messages only.

      -Q   restore default condition changed by **-q**. Print compilation statistics and warn of unusual constructs.

      -r   place bootstrap code at the beginning of the object file. This invokes a LISP system when the object file is executed.

      -S   compile *pfile* and leave the assembler-language output on the corresponding file suffixed **.s**. The assembler language file will not be assembled.

-T	send the assembler output to standard output.	**liszt** *continued*
-u	compile a UCI-lispfile by converting to UCI-LISP syntax. Similar to **-m**.	
-w	suppress warning diagnostics.	
-x	create a lisp cross-reference file with a **.x** suffix. **lxref** can then create a readable listing.	

ln [*options*] *files* [*target*]   **ln**

Create a pseudonym (link) for *file* named *target*. If more than one file is specified and *target* is an existing directory, then *files* are linked into *target*.

options

   -f   force link to occur without questions.

   -s   create a symbolic link. This option is valid across filesystems.

lock [*options*]   **lock**

Lock, or reserve, a terminal. After the user types the requested password, the terminal is locked until the password is repeated, or until a time limit is reached.

options

   -n   change time limit to *n* minutes (default = 15).

logger [*options*] [*string*]   **logger**

Enter *string* into system log. If *string* is omitted, entry is taken from standard input. End with ^**D**.

options

   -t*tag*   mark each line in the log with *tag*.

   -p*priority*
          enter message with specified *priority*.

   -i   enter process id with each line.

   -f*file* log *file*.

login	**login** [*user*]
	Sign on and identify yourself to the system. At the beginning of each terminal session, the system prompts you for your *user* name and, optionally, a password.
look	**look** [*options*] *string* [*file*]
	Search a sorted *file* and print all lines beginning with *string*.
	options
	-d dictionary order.
	-f ignore upper/lower case distinction.
lookbib	**lookbib** [*options*] *database*
	Interactively search a bibliographic database. See also **refer** and **indxbib**.
	options
	-n do not prompt for instructions.
lorder	**lorder** *files*
	List pairs of object file names. The **lorder** output can be sent to **tsort** to create a random library.
lpq	**lpq** [*options*] [*job#s*] [*users*]
	List the name, id number, and size of the files that are queued for printing. You can query the status of a particular *job#*, or all jobs belonging to a particualr *user*.
	options
	-l print information about the files associated with *job*.
	-P*printer*
	report information on *printer*.
	+[*n*] display spool queue. Sleep *n* seconds and scan again.

lpr [*options*] [*files*] **lpr**

Queue one or more *files* for printing.

options

-#*n*   print *n* copies of *files*.

-c   use the **cifplot** filter.

-C*class*
        print the class name *class* on the first page output.

-d   use the **tex** filter.

-f   use the first character for FORTRAN style carriage control.

-g   use the **plot** filter.

-h   do not print the burst page.

-i [*num*]
        indent the output 8 or *n* spaces.

-J*jobn*
        print the jobname *jobn* on the first page output.

-l   use filter printing control characters and suppressing page breaks.

-m   send mail upon completion.

-n   use the **ditroff** filter.

-p   format the files with **pr**.

-P*printer*
        send output to the printer named *printer*.

-r   remove the file after it is copied to the spool directory.

-s   link rather than copy the files to the spool directory.

-t   use the **troff** filter.

-T *title* print *title* as the title for **pr**.

-v   use the **rasterfile** filter.

-w*n*   use a page width of *n* for the **pr** command.

-1*font* mount *font* on position 1.

-2*font* mount *font* on position 2.

-3*font* mount *font* on position 3.

-4*font* mount *font* on position 4.

---

lprm [*options*] [*job#s*] [*user*] **lprm**

Remove a job currently printing. *user* must have issued the print command for the job. *job#s* may be listed with **lpq**.

☞

lprm
 continued
	options
	      - remove all print jobs for the user issuing the command.
	      -P*printer*
	          remove the requests associated with the printer named *printer*.

lptest	**lptest** [*length* [*n*]] Print all 96 printable ASCII characters in each position on the standard output. Specify output line length to be *length* (default = 79), and the number of output lines to be *n* (default = 200).
ls	**ls** [*options*] [*directory*] List the files contained in the current or specified *directory*. *options*

For the **ls** command options:

-1	list one entry per line.
-a	list all files including "." files.
-c	list by file creation/modification time.
-C	list multicolumn output to a file or pipe.
-d	list only directory name, not its contents.
-f	interpret each argument as a directory.
-F	append "/" to directories and "*" to executable files.
-g	list group id in long listing.
-i	list i-nodes for each file.
-l	long format listing.
-L	list the directory associated with a symbolic link.
-q	show non-printing characters as "?".
-r	list in reverse order.
-R	recursively list subdirectories as well as current directory.
-s	print size of the files in blocks.
-t	list files according to the file modification dates.
-u	list files according to the file access time.

lxref [-N]*file* [*options*]   **lxref**

Lisp cross reference program. **lxref** reads *file* written by **liszt**, the LISP compiler. A cross-reference listing is then printed on the standard output.

options

-*N*   if a function is called more than *N* times, the cross reference listing prints the number of calls rather than listing each one (default = 50).

-**a** *sourcefile*
        put limited cross-reference information in the named sources.

---

m4 [*options*] [*files*]   **m4**

Macro processor for RATFOR, C, and other programs.

options

-**B***n*   set push-back argument collection buffers to *n* (default is 4,096).

-**D***name*[=*value*]
        define *name* to *value* or null if *value* is not specified.

-**e**   operate interactively.

-**H***n*   set symbol table hash array to *n*.

-**s**   enable line sync output.

-**S***n*   set call stack size to *n* (default is 100 slots).

-**T***n*   set token buffer size to *n* (default is 512 bytes).

-**U***name*
        undefine *name*.

---

mail [*options*] [*users*]   **mail**

Read mail and send mail to other *users*. Type ? for a summary of commands.

options

-**e**   do not print mail. Exit with status 0 if mail exists, otherwise exit with status 1.

-**f** [*file*]
        read *file* for mail messages.

☞

---

mail
continued

-H	print the mail headers only.
-i	ignore interrupts.
-n	do not read the **Mail.rc** file.
-s *subject*	
	specify *subject*.
-u *user*	
	read *user*'s mail.
-v	display details of delivery.

make

make [*options*] [*targets*]

Update one or more targets according to the list of dependencies located in a file called **Makefile** or *makefile* in the current directory. See Section 9 for more information on **make**.

options

-b	compatibility mode for old versions of makefiles.
-d	print detailed debugging information.
-e	override makefile assignments with environment variables.
-f *makefile*	
	override default rules (**Makefile**) with *makefile* (or .DEFAULT).
-i	ignore command error codes (or .IGNORE).
-k	abandon work on current entry; continue with unrelated entries.
-m	print a memory map.
-n	print commands, but do not execute.
-p	print macro definitions and makefile descriptions.
-q	return 0 if file is up to date or non-zero if it is not.
-r	do not use "default" rules.
-s	do not print command lines (.SILENT in description file).
-t	touch the target files, causing them to be updated.

man [*options*] [*section*] *subject*   **man**

Print the page in the *UNIX Programmer's Manual* that
describes *subject*. *subject* is assumed to be a command as described in Section 1, unless you specify an
optional *section* from 1 to 8.

options

-     pipe output through **more -s**.
- **-f** *file* display **man** sections related to *file*.
- **-k** *keyword*
      print manual section headings containing
      keyword.
- **-m***path*
      search *path* for description of *subject*.
- **-P***path*
      search for man files in the directory named
      path.
- **-t**   format the section with **troff**.

---

mesg [*options*]   **mesg**

Print the current state of write permission on your terminal. The permission is changed with the specified
options.

options

  n   forbid **write** messages.
  y   allow **write** messages (default).

---

mh   **mh**

Read mail using the **mh** message handling system.
mh has many subsidiary commands. To get started,
use **inc** to set up default files. The following commands are supported:

mh commands

  ali   List mail aliases.
  anno Annotate messages.
  burst Explode digests into messages.
  comp Compose a message.
  dist Redistribute a message to additional
      addresses.

☞

mh
continued

folder Set/list current folder/message.

folders
List all folders.

forw Forward messages.

inc Incorporate new mail.

mark Mark messages.

mhl Produce formatted listings of **mh** messages.

mhmail
Send or read mail.

mhook
mh receive-mail hooks.

mhpath
Print full pathnames of **mh** messages and folders.

msgchk
Check for messages.

msh mh shell and BBoard reader.

next Show the next message.

packf Compress a folder into a single file.

pick Select messages by content.

prev Show the previous message.

prompter
Prompting editor front end.

rcvstore
Incorporate new mail asynchronously.

refile File messages in other folders.

repl Reply to a message.

rmf Remove folder.

rmm Remove messages.

scan Produce a one line per message scan listing.

send Send a message.

show Show (list) messages.

sortm Sort messages.

vmh Visual front-end to **mh**.

whatnow
Prompting front-end for send.

whom Report to whom a message should go.

Use the **-help** option with any of these commands for more details.

mkdir *directories* Create one or more *directories*. You must have write permission in the parent directory in order to create a directory.	**mkdir**
mkstr [*options*] *messagefile prefix files* Extract error messages from C source *files*; place messages in *messagefile*, and place processed copies of each source file in a file of the same name, but beginning with *prefix*. *options* - place error messages at end of *messagefile*.	**mkstr**
more [*options*] [*files*] Display the named *files* on a terminal, one page at a time. After each screen is displayed, you are prompted to display the next line, by pressing the RETURN key, or the next screenful of text, by pressing the SPACE BAR. For additional commands, press **h** for help. This command can also be invoked using the name **page**. *options* **-c** overwrite lines. **-d** prompt for "Hit space to continue, Rubout to abort". **-f** count logical rather than screen lines. **-l** ignore formfeed (^L) characters. **-***n* use *n* lines for each window (default is a full screen). **+***n* begin displaying at line number *n*. **-s** display multiple blank lines as one. **-u** suppress backspace (^H) and underline characters. **+/***pattern* begin displaying two lines before *pattern*.	**more**
mount [*special*] [*dir*] Report the status of mounted special files. When this command is issued with *special* device and *dir*	**mount** ☞

mount *continued*	arguments, the *special* device is mounted on *dir*. **umount** *special* unmounts a special device. Options are system specific.
mset	**mset** Retrieve keyboard mapping from ASCII to IBM 3270 terminal.
msgs	**msgs** [*options*] [*mnum*] [*-n*] A program to read system messages. Normally, **msgs** is invoked at login. *options* <ul><li>**-c**[*-days*] remove all messages over 21 days old.</li><li>**-f** suppress printing of the phrase, "No new messages."</li><li>**-h** print first part of message only.</li><li>**-l** report messages of local origin only.</li><li>**-p** pipe long messages through **more**.</li><li>**-q** query whether there are messages. If so, the phrase, "There are new messages." is printed.</li><li>**-s** set up posting of messages.</li><li>*mnum* start at the specified message number *mnum* instead of the one shown by the **.msgrc** file.</li><li>**-n** Start *n* messages back from the one indicated by the **.msgrc** file.</li></ul>
mt	**mt** [**-f** *tapename*] *mtcommands* [*n*] Send *mtcommands* *n* times to the magnetic tape drive (default = 1). If device name *tapename* is not specified, **/dev/rmt12** is used. *options* <ul><li>**-f** use tapename as the specified device (default **/dev/nrmt0**).</li></ul>

eof,weof
> write count end-of-file marks.

fsf   space forward *count* files.

fsr   space forward *count* records.

bsf   space back *count* files.

bsr   space back *count* records.

rew   rewind the tape.

status print status information about the tape unit.

offl   rewind tape and go offline.

erase erase entire tape cartridge.

retension
> re-tension the tape cartridge.

reset reset the tape drive.

---

mv [*options*] *file target*

mv

Move (or rename) *file* to *target*, or move one or more *files* to the existing directory *target*.

options

-    all arguments which follow are file or directory names. This includes names beginning with "-".

-f   force mode, suppress error messages.

-i   request interactive confirmation of each move.

---

neqn [*options*] [*files*]

neqn

Numerical equation preprocessor for **nroff**. Use **eqn** with **troff**. See Section 7 for more information on **eqn**.

options

-d*xy*   use *x* and *y* as start and stop delimiters.

-f*n*   change to font *n*.

-p*n*   reduce the superscript size by *n* points.

-s*n*   reduce the point size by *n* points.

---

netstat

netstat [*options*] [*system*] [*core*]

Symbolically display network status. Specify *system*
and *core* to substitute for the default **/vmunix** and
/dev/kmem.

options

-a   show the state of all sockets.

-A   show the address of any associated protocol control blocks.

-f *address_fam*
limit statistics or reports to those of
address_fam. Recognized address families
are:

inet   AF_INET
ns   AF_NS
unix   AF_UNIX

-h   show the state of the IMP host table.

-i   show the state of interfaces which have
been auto-configured.

-I *interface n*
show information only about specified
interface at every interval *n*.

-m   show statistics recorded by the memory
management routines.

-n   show network addresses as numbers
instead of symbolically.

-p *protocol*
show the state of sockets utilizing *protocol*,
which is specified symbolically.

-r   show routing tables.

-s   show per-protocol statistics.

interval
continuously display packet traffic information, refreshing the screen every *interval*
seconds.

newaliases

newaliases

Rebuild the random access data base for the mail
aliases file **/usr/lib/aliases**.

nice *[options] command [arguments]*   **nice**

Execute a *command* and *arguments* with low priority.

options

  -n   (Bourne Shell only.) Run *command* with a niceness of *n* (1-19). The higher the niceness number, the lower the priority. {Default = 4}

  -n   (C Shell only.) Run *command* with a niceness of negative *n*. This raises the priority. Only the superuser may do this.

  +n   (C Shell only.) Run *command* with a niceness of *n*. This lowers the priority.

  --n   (Bourne Shell only.) Run *command* with a niceness of negative *n*. This raises the priority. Only the superuser may do this.

---

nm *[options] [files]*   **nm**

Print the symbol table (name list) in alphabetical order for one or more *files*.

options

  -a   include all symbols.
  -g   print only external symbols.
  -n   sort numerically.
  -o   prepend source filename to each line.
  -p   print in symbol table order.
  -r   sort in reverse order.
  -u   print only undefined symbols.

symbol values

  A   absolute symbol.
  B   bss segment symbol.
  C   common symbol.
  D   data segment symbol.
  f   file name.
  T   text segment symbol.
  U   undefined symbol.
  -   debug symbol entries.

nohup	**nohup** *command* [*arguments*] **&**

Continue to execute the named *command* and optional command *arguments* after you log out (make command immune to hangups).

notes	**notes** [*options*] *notesfiles*

Access or update a database of notes and responses broadcast over Usenet. This interface can be used instead of the **readnews** or **vnews** programs.

options

    -s   use the sequencer.

    -x   use the sequencer and enter files even if there is no new text.

    -i   use the sequencer but show index page instead of first note.

    -n   do not use sequencer.

    -o*datespec*
        find article matching *datespec*.

    -a*subseq*
        specify a subsequencer.

    -t*ttytype*
        override TERM environment variable with *ttytype*.

    -f*file* read *file* for list of notesfiles to scan.

nroff	**nroff** [*options*] [*files*]

Format one or more text *files* for printing. See Section 5 for more information on **nroff**.

options

    -e   space words equally.

    -h   use tabs in large spaces.

    -i   read standard input after files are processed.

    -m*name*
        prepend **/usr/lib/tmac/tmac.***name* to files.

    -n*n*   number first page *n*.

    -o*list* print only pages contained in *list*. A page range is specified by *n-m*.

    -q   invoke simultaneous input-output of **.rd** requests.

-r *an*	set register *a* to *n*.	**nroff**
-s *n*	stop every *n* pages.	*continued*
-T *name*		
	output is for device type *name*.	

---

od [*options*] [*file*] [[+][*offset*[.][**b**] [*label*]]   **od**

Produce an octal dump of the named *file*.

options

-a	display bytes as characters.
-b	display bytes as octal.
-c	display bytes as ASCII.
-d	display words as decimal.
-f	display words as floating point.
-h	display short words as hexadecimal.
-i	display short words as decimal.
-l	display long words as signed decimal.
-o	display words as octal (the default).
-s[*n*]	display character strings terminated by a null character with a minimum length of *n*.
-v	display all data.
-w[*n*]	display *n* input bytes per line.
-x	display short words as hexadecimal.
+	required if *file* not specified.
offset	start dumping *file* at octal offset.
.	decimal offset.
b	offset in 512-byte blocks.
label	pseudo-address for first byte displayed.

---

pagesize   **pagesize**

Print the size of a page of memory in bytes.

---

passwd [*user*]   **passwd**

Create or change a password associated with a *user* name (current user is default). Only the owner or superuser may change a password.

options

-f	change GECOS information field.
-s	change the login shell.

---

patch

patch [*options*] *file patchfile* [+[*options*] *file*]

Apply differences listed in *patchfile* to *file*, placing the original version of *file* in *file*.**orig**. *patchfile* is in any of the three forms created by **diff**.

options

-b*SUFFIX*
    place original version of file in *fileSUFFIX*.

-c   interpret *patchfile* as a context **diff** file.

-d*dir* change directory to *dir* before proceeding.

-D   use **#ifdef ... endef** construct to mark changes.

-e   interpret *patchfile* as an **ed** script.

-l   perform pattern-matching loosely.

-n   interpret *patchfile* as a normal **diff** file.

-N   do not reverse diffs.

-o*name*
    place output in *file*.

-p   keep leading pathnames.

-r*file* take *file* as reject file name.

-R   *patchfile* was created with old and new files swapped.

-s   silent mode, unless an error is encountered.

-x<*n***>** set internal debugging flags.

pc

pc [*options*] *files*.**p**

Compile *file*.**p** in Pascal and create executable file (**a.out** by default).

options

-b   block buffer the output.

-c   suppress compilation loading and produce **.o** files.

-C   compile code to initialize all variables to 0, perform **runtime** checks, and verify **assert** calls.

-g   create additional symbol table information.

-i   list specified procedures, functions, and **include** files.

-l   list programs during translation.

-O   invoke object code optimizer.

-p   set up object files for profiling.

-s	accept standard Pascal only.	**pc**
-S	produce assembler **.s** files.	*continued*
-t*dir*	place compiler temporary files in *dir*.	
-w	suppress warning messages.	
-z	allow execution profiling by **pxp**.	

---

pdx [*options*] [*objfile*]   **pdx**

Debug and execute Pascal programs. *objfile* is an
object file created by **pi**.

options

    -r   execute *objfile* immediately.

---

pi *options file*.**p**   **pi**

Produce Pascal interpreter code and send output to
a.out.

options

    -b   buffer the output.

    -i*files* specify functions, procedures, or **include**
           files.

    -l   produce a listing.

    -L   use only lower case for function and proce-
           dure names.

    -n   output a new page for each include file.

    -o*name*
           sent output to *name*.

    -p   suppress backtrace on error.

    -s   produce warning messages for non-stan-
           dard Pascal.

    -t   suppress runtime checking of subranges.

    -u   use only 72 characters per line.

    -w   supress all warning messages.

    -z   create the profiling data file **pmon.out** for
           pxp.

---

pix [*options*] *file*.**p** [*arguments*]   **pix**

Translate and execute Pascal interpreter code. This
program uses **pi** to translate the code and **px** to execute it.

☞

---

pix *continued*	*options* All of the **pi** options are available.

plot	**plot** [*options*] [*files*]
	
	Produce plotting instructions from the commands on standard input.
	options
	  -T *terminal*
	      specify output for *terminal*. Several valid *terminals* can be specified.
	  -r*resl* specify device's output resolution as *resl*.

pmerge	**pmerge** *files*.**p** Create a single Pascal file from a collection of single files.
pr	**pr** [*options*] [*files*] Format one or more *files* according to *options*. Each page includes a heading that consists of the page number, filename, date, and time. *options*

options

-f	use form feed (^L) character instead of a series of newlines to separate pages.
-h *string*	replace default header with *string*. Set page length to *n* (default is 66).
-l*n*	set page length to *n* (default is 66).
-m	merge the files and print them, one file in each column (overrides -k and -a).
+*n*	begin printing at page *n* (default is 1).
-*n*	produce output with *n*-columns (default is 1).
-s*c*	separate columns with *c* (default is a tab).
-t	omit the page header and trailer.
-w*n*	set line width to *n* (default is 72 for equal width multicolumn output).

printenv [*variable*] Print the values of all variables in the environment or, optionally, only the specified *variable*.	**printenv**
prmail [*user*] Print the mail waiting for you or for *user*.	**prmail**

prof [*options*] [*objfile* [*pfile*]]

Display the profile data for object file *objfile*. Default object file is **a.out** and default profile file is **mon.out**, unless specified otherwise.

options

    -a   report all symbols.
    -l   list by symbol value.
    -n   list by number of calls
    -s   produce a summary **mon.sum**.
    -v[*-m*[*-n*]]
            graphic version of the profile. Plot the low (*m*) and high (*n*) percentage limits with higher resolution (defaults are 0 and 100).
    -z   include zero usage calls.

prof

---

prs [*options*] *files*

Print all or portions of one or more SCCS *files*. For more information on SCCS, see Section 9.

options

    -a   print information for removed deltas.

prs

---

ps [*options*]

Report on active processes.

options

    -a   all processes except group leaders and processes not associated with a terminal.
    -c   print command names without arguments.
    -e   print the environment associated with a command.

ps

☞

ps *continued*	**-g** print all processes including group leaders. **-k** change the default kernel name, dump file, and swap file. **-l** print the long listing. **-n** print numerical output. **-s** output a column for the SSIZ of the kernel stack. **-t***tty* print processes associated with terminal *tty*. This option must be specified last. **-u***user* print processes associated with *user*. **-U** update database with system information. **-v** print output including a virtual memory field. **-w** print output in the wide format. **-x** print processes without terminals. **-***n* print information about process *n*. This must be the last option specified.

ptx	**ptx** [*options* [*file1* [*file2*]]]
	
	Generate a permuted index of *file1* into *file2*. Files must be formatted with **nroff -mptx** to actually produce the index. If files are not specified, standard input and output are used.
	
	options
	
	   -b*file* use characters in *file* to separate words.
	   -f sort with no upper/lower case distinction.
	   -g *n* change the space between columns to *n* (default is 3).
	   -i *file* ignore the keywords in *file*.
	   -o *file* use only the words in *file*.
	   -r use first field in *ifile* as fifth field (non-permuted reference id) in *ofile*.
	   -t prepare the output to be phototypeset.
	   -w *n* change the line length to *n* (default is 72).

pwd	**pwd** Print the full pathname of the current directory. (In the C Shell, the built-in command **dirs** is much faster.)

px [*objfile* [*arguments*]]	**px**
Interpret Pascal object code.	

pxp [*options*] *file*.**p**   **pxp**

Format or profile a Pascal program.

options

-**a**   include all procedures and functions.
-**c**   use **core** file for the profile data.
-**d**   include declarations.
-**e**   remove the include statements and replace
         with the contents of the include files.
-**f**   fully parenthesize expressions.
-**j**   left justify procedures and functions.
-**L**   use only lower case for keywords and iden-
         tifiers.
-**n**   use new pages for include files.
-**s**   remove comments.
-**t**   produce procedure and function call
         counts.
-**u**   use only the first 72 characters on each
         line.
-**w**   suppress warning messages.
-**z**name ...
         produce the execution profile for all func-
         tions and procedures, or for the functions
         and procedures with the specified *names*.
-_   underline keywords.
-n indent n spaces for pretty format, $2 \le n \le 9$
         (default = 4).

pxref *options file*   **pxref**

Produce a listing and cross-reference for Pascal source
file.

options

-       do not print the listing.

quota [*options*] [*user*]   **quota**

Report disk usage and quota information. Only a
super-user may request information about other users.

☞

quota
continued
	options
	    -q limit the display to filesystems where the quota is exceeded.
	    -v print the verbose display with information about all filesystems.

ranlib	**ranlib** [*options*] *archives* Convert *archives* into a random library which can be rapidly loaded. *options* **-t** only touch archive, do not modify.

ratfor	**ratfor** [*options*] [*files*]
	
	Convert rational FORTRAN to irrational FORTRAN.
	options
	    -C retain comments in the translated version.
	    -h convert strings to Hollerith constants.
	    -6*c* change the continuation character to *c*.

rcp	**rcp** [*options*] *source(s) target*
	
	Copy files between machines. Both *sources* and *target* are filename specifications of the form *host:pathname*, where *host:* can be omitted for a file on the local machine.
	options
	    -p preserve in copies the modification times and modes of the source files.
	    -r if *target* and *sources* are both directories, copy each subtree rooted in the source.

rdist	**rdist** [*options*] [*files*] Maintain identical copies of files over multiple hosts. *options* **-n** print commands but do not execute.

-q	quiet mode: do not print files on standard output.	**rdist** _continued_
-b	perform a binary comparison and update files if they differ.	
-R	remove extra files.	
-h	follow symbolic links.	
-i	ignore unresolved links.	
-v	verify that _files_ are up to date on all hosts.	
-w	append whole file name to destination directory name.	
-y	do not update files younger than the master copy.	
-f _file_	update all files and directories listed in _file_.	
-d _var=val_		
	define or override variable definitions.	
-m _machine_		
	update only the machine listed. This option may be used repeatedly.	
-c	interpret all remaining arguments as files listing files and directories to be updated.	

---

readnews [_options_]

Print unread articles posted over the Usenet.

options

    -a _date_
        all articles posted past given _date_.
    -n _groups_
        all articles belonging to _groups_.
    -t _strings_
        all articles containing one of the specified _strings_.

-l	only output titles, do not update file.
-e	only output titles, but also update file.
-p	send all articles selected to standard output.
-r	print articles in reverse order.
-x	select articles that have already been read as well as new ones.
-h	print articles in less verbose format, at 300 baud.
-f	do not print follow-up articles.
-u	update **.newsrc** file every five minutes.

readnews

☞

readnews *continued*	**-M** mail interface. **-c** [*mailer*] **binmail** interface. If *mailer* is specified, write all selected articles to temporary file and invoke *mailer*. **-s** print the newsgroup subscription list.

---

refer

refer [*options*] [*files*]

Preprocessor for **nroff** and **troff** to find and format references.

options

-a [*n*]   reverse all or the first *n* author's names.

-b   omit numbers and labels in text.

-B*l.m*   bibliography mode.

-c *string*
       capitalize fields whose key letters are in *string*.

-e   accumulate references and write at the sequence:
       .[
       $LIST$
       .]

-f*n*   set footnote number to *n* (default = 1).

-k*x*   use labels in a reference data line beginning with %*x* (default is L).

-l [*m,n*]
       use author's last name and publication date for references. Only the first *m* letters of the last name and the last *n* digits of the date are used.

-n   do not search the default file.

-p*file*   search *file* before the default file.

-P   place punctuation marks after reference signal instead of before.

-s *string*
       sort references by fields whose key letters are in *string*.

-S   use Natural or Social Science format.

rev [*files*]   **rev**

Reverse the order of the characters in each line of one or more *files*, in effect creating a mirror image of the text.

---

rlogin *host* [*options*]   **rlogin**

Connect terminal on current local host system to remote host system *host*.

options

-e *c*   specify escape character as *c* (default = ˜).
-8   allow eight-bit input data path.
-L   run **rlogin** session in litout mode.

---

rm [*options*] *files*   **rm**

Delete one or more *files*. To remove a file, you must have write permission in the directory that contains the file, but you need not have permission on the file itself. If you do not have write permission on the file, you will be prompted (**y** or **n**) to override.

options

-f   remove files unconditionally.
-i   prompt for "y" yes remove the file or "n" do not remove the file.
-r   if *file* is a directory, remove the entire directory and all its contents, including subdirectories. (Use of this option can be very dangerous.)
-       use this option before a list of filenames which includes a filename beginning with "-".

---

rmdel *options files*   **rmdel**

Remove a delta from one or more SCCS *files*. See also **sccs**; for more information on SCCS, see Section 9.

options

-r *sid*   the SCCS id version number.

---

rmdir	**rmdir** *directories*
	Delete entries for *directories*. *directories* must be empty. They are deleted from the parent directory. To remove a directory that is not empty, use **rm -r**.
roffbib	**roffbib** [*options*] [*database*]
	Print all records from *database*.
	options

options

- **-e**   space words equally.
- **-h**   use tabs in large spaces.
- **-m** *name*
        prepend **/usr/lib/tmac/tmac.***name* to files.
- **-n** *n*   number first page *n*.
- **-o** *list*   print only pages contained in *list*. A page range is specified by *n-m*.
- **-Q**   send output to the phototypesetter.
- **-r** *an*   set register *a* to *n*.
- **-s** *n*   stop every *n* pages.
- **-T** *term*
        output is for device type *term*.
- **-V**   send output to the Versatec.
- **-x**   format %X fields as paragraphs.

rsh	**rsh** *host* [*options*] [*command*]
	Connect to *host* and execute *command*. If *command* is not specified, **rsh** allows you to **rlogin** to *host*.

options

- **-l** *username*
        connect to *host* as user *username*.
- **-n**   divert input to **/dev/null**.

ruptime	**ruptime** [*options*]
	Show the status of local networked machines.

options

- **-a**   do not overlook users idle more than 1 hour.
- **-r**   reverse the sort order.

-l	sort by load average.	**ruptime**
-t	sort by uptime.	*continued*
-u	sort by number of users.	

---

rwho [*options*]   **rwho**

Report who is logged on for all machines on local network.

options

  -a   do not overlook users idle more than 1 hour.

---

sact *files*   **sact**

Print the current editing activity for one or more SCCS *files*.

---

sccs [*options*] *command* [*flags*] [*files*]   **sccs**

Provide access to all SCCS commands and files without the need for the "**s.**" extension. By default the subdirectory SCCS contains the **s.** files. **sccs** provides the pseudo SCCS commands listed below. For more information on SCCS, see Section 9.

options

  -d*prepath*
        use *prepath* in place of the current directory as the source of *file*.
  -p*endpath*
        use *endpath* as the directory containing *file*.
  -r   use *sccs* identified by your real username rather than your *user id*.

sccs commands

admin, cdc, comb, delta, get, help, prs, rmdel, sact, sccsdiff, unget, val, what

sccs pseudo-commands

admin, check, clean, create, deledit, delget, diffs, edit, fix, info, tell, unedit

---

sccsdiff	**sccsdiff** -r*sid1* -r*sid2* [*options*] [*diffopts*] *files*
	Report the differences of two versions of an SCCS *file*. See also **sccs**; for more information on SCCS, see Section 9.
	options
	-diffopts
	diff options **-b**, **-c**, **-D**, **-e**, **-f**, and **-h**, can follow the *sccsdiff* options.
	-p pipe output through **pr**.
	-r*sidn* compare deltas of *sid1* with *sid2*.
	-s*n* file segment size is *n*.
script	**script** [*options*] [*file*]
	Copy all output displayed on the terminal to *file*.
	options
	-a append the output to *file*.
sed	**sed** [*options*] [*files*]
	Edit one or more *files* using the commands listed from *files* or from standard input. See Section 4 for more information on **sed**.
	options
	-e *script*
	execute commands in *script*.
	-f*file* take script from *file*.
	-n suppress default output.
sendbug	**sendbug** [*address*]
	Mail bug reports in the correct format. Bugs are sent to "4bsd-bugs@Berkeley.EDU" unless otherwise specified.
sh	**sh** [*options*] [*commands*]
	The standard command interpreter which executes *commands* from a terminal or a file. See section 2 for more information on **sh**.

options

    -c *string*

        read commands from *string*.

    -s   read commands from standard input.

    -i   interactive shell; ignore terminate and interrupt signals.

sh
continued

---

shutdown [*options*] [*time*]

Terminate all processes and take system down to single-user mode. The format of *time* and the options are system specific.

options

    -h   execute halt.

    -k   issue **shutdown** messages, but do not shutdown the system.

    -r   execute reboot.

shutdown

---

size [*objfile* ...]

Print the (decimal) number of bytes of each *objfile*. If *objfile* is not specified, **a.out** is used.

size

---

sleep *seconds*

Wait for a specified number of *seconds*.

sleep

---

soelim [*files*]

Eliminate the **.so** commands (see **nroff**) from *file* and perform the implied textual inclusion.

soelim

---

sort [*options*] [*files*]

Sort the lines of the named *files* in alphabetical order.

options

    -b   ignore leading spaces and tabs.

    -c   verify the input file.

    -d   sort in dictionary order.

sort

☞

sort *continued*	**-f**	fold upper to lower case.
	-i	ignore characters outside the ASCII 040-176 range.
	-m	merge sorted input files.
	-n	sort an initial numeric string by arithmetic value.
	-o*file*	place output in *file*.
	-r	reverse the sense of comparisons.
	-t*c*	use *c* as the tab character separating fields.
	-T *dir*	place **sort** temporary files in the directory *dir*.
	-u	print only unique lines.
	+*pos1* [*-pos2*]	
		restrict sort key starting at *pos1* and ending at *pos2*, *pos1* and *pos2* of the form *m.n*, *m* specifying number of fields to skip from beginning of the line and *n* specifying the number of characters to skip after that.

---

sortbib

sortbib [*options*] *databases*

Sort a file of **refer** records by user-specified keys.

options

    -s*keys*

        the specified *keys* control the sort fields.

---

spell

spell [*options*] [*files*]

Compare the words of one or more named *files* with the system dictionary and report all misspelled words.

options

    -v   print all words not literally in spelling list; indicate plausible derivations.

    -b   check for British spelling.

    -x   print every plausible stem with "=" for each word.

    -d*file* use *file* as an auxiliary spelling list.

    -s*file* use *file* as an auxiliary stop list.

    -h*file* use *file* as an auxiliary history file.

spline [*options*]   **spline**

Create a "smooth" function from the *x-y* coordinates
given as number pairs via standard input. The output
is also a set of *x-y* coordinates, which can be plotted
with **graph** and **plot**. A maximum of 1000 points can
be specified.

options

-a   add abscissas automatically.
-k*n*   use *n* for the constant value in the bound-
        ary computation.
-*n*   use *n* intervals between the upper and
        lower x-limits.
-p   create periodic output.
-x*low* [*up*]
        lower and upper x-limits.

---

split [*options*] [*ifile*] [*ofile*]   **split**

Split *ifile* into a specified number of line segments and
write the results to *ofile*aa, *ofile*bb, etc. (Default is
xaa, xab, etc.)

options

-*n*   split *ifile* into *n* line segments (default is
        1000).

---

strings *files*   **strings**

Search one or more *files* (usually binary) for
sequences of four or more printable characters that end
with a newline or null.

options

-       search entire *file*.
-o   precede each string with its offset.
-*n*   minimum string length is *n* (default is 4).

---

strip [*options*] *files*   **strip**

Remove the symbol table and relocation bits from
object files *files*.

struct	**struct** [*options*] *file*

Translate a FORTRAN program into a RATFOR program.

options

- **-a** change all "else if" statements into non-RATFOR switches.
- **-b** use "go to" statements in place of multilevel breaks.
- **-c***n* increment labels in output by *n* (default is 1).
- **-e***n* *n*=0 place code within loop, *n*>0 admit small code segments to loop.
- **-i** do not turn computed "go to" statements into switches.
- **-n** use "go to" statements in place of multilevel next statements.
- **-s** accept input in the standard format.
- **-t***n* make *n* the lowest valued label in the output program (default is 10).

stty	**stty** [*options*]

Set terminal I/O options for the current device. Without options, **stty** reports the terminal settings. As superuser, you can set or read settings from another device using the syntax:

stty [*options*] < *device*

options

all report all options.
everything
    print all information.
speed print terminal speed.
size print terminal sizes (rows, columns).

mode-setting options

0 hang up phone.
even allow even parity input.
-even do not allow even parity input.
odd allow odd parity input.
-odd do not allow odd parity input.
raw raw mode input.

-raw   no raw mode input.
cooked
>   no raw mode input.

cbreak
>   make each character available to **read** as processed.

-cbreak
>   make each character available to **read** only at newline.

-nl   all carriage return for newline.
nl   allow only newline for newline.
echo   echo each character typed.
-echo do not echo characters.
lcase map upper case to lower case.
-lcase do not map upper case to lower case.
tandem
>   enable flow control.

-tandem
>   disable flow control.

-tabs replace tabs with spaces.
tabs   do not replace tabs.

Control character settings

Character arguments c may be specified as "**u**" to set the value as undefined.

ek   set *erase* to # and *kill* to @.
erase c
>   set erase character to c (default #).

kill c set kill character to c (default @).
intr c set interrupt character to c (default DEL).
quit c set quit character to c (default CTRL-\).
start c set start character to c (default CTRL-Q).
stop c set stop character to c (default CTRL-S).
eof c set end of file character to c (default CTRL-D).
brk c set break character to c (default undefined).
cr$n$ set style of delay for carriage return to n, $0 \le n \ 3$.
nl$n$ set style of delay for linefeed to n, $0 \le n \le 3$.
tab$n$ set style of delay for tab to n, $0 \le n \le 3$.
ff$n$ set style of delay for form feed to n, $n = 0$ or 1.

bs*n*   set style of delay for backspace to *n*, *n* = 0 or 1.

Terminal modes

tty33   set modes suitable for Teletype Model 33 terminal.

tty37   set modes suitable for Teletype Model 37 terminal.

vt05   set modes suitable for DEC VT05 terminal.

dec   set modes suitable for DEC operating systems users.

tn300   set modes suitable for GE TermiNet 300.

ti700   set modes suitable for TI 700 series terminal.

tek   set modes suitable for Tektronix 4014 terminal.

n   set terminal baud rate to *n*. Possible values for *n*: 50, 75, 110, 134, 150, 200, 300, 600, 1200, 1800, 2400, 4800, 9600, exta, extb.

rows *n*
record terminal size as having *n* rows.

cols   record terminal size as having *n* columns.

Teletype modes

These options apply only to teletype drivers which support job control processing of **csh** and enhanced functionality.

new   use new driver.

crt   set modes for a CRT.

crtbs   echo backspace on erase characters.

prterase
echo "/" and "\" for erase characters (for printing terminal).

crterase
wipe out erased characters with "backspace-space-backspace".

-crterase
do not wipe out erase characters.

crtkill wipe out "killed" lines with "backspace-space-backspace".

-crtkill
only echo kill character and a newline on line kill.

ctlecho
> echo control characters as "^x" and delete as "^?". Print two backspaces following CTRL-D.

-ctlecho
> echo control characters as themselves.

decctlq
> only *start* character will restart output that has been suspended.

-decctlq
> any character will restart output that has been suspended (default).

tostop background jobs will stop upon attempting output to terminal.

-tostop
> allow output to terminal from background jobs.

tilde convert "˜" to "˜" on output.

-tilde do not convert tildes.

flusho discard output upon using CTRL-O.

-flusho
> do not discard output on CTRL-O.

pendin
> input is pending after **cbreak** switch to cooked.

-pendin
> input is not pending.

pass8 pass all 8 bits through on input.

-pass8
> strip 0200 bit on input except raw mode.

mdmbuf
> start or stop output on carrier transitions.

-mdmbuf
> return error if write is attempted after carrier drops.

litout send output characters without processing.

-litout perform normal output processing.

nohang
> do not send output processing if carrier drops.

-nohang
> send hangup signal if carrier drops.

etxack
> use etx/ack handshaking.

☞

stty
continued
	susp *c* set suspend process character to *c* (default CTRL-Z).
	dsusp *c*
	    set delayed suspend process character to *c* (default CTRL-Y).
	rprnt *c*set reprint line character to *c* (default CTRL-R).
	flush *c*
	    set flush output character to *c* (default CTRL-O).
	werase *c*
	    set word erase character to *c* (default CTRL-W).
	lnext *c*
	    set literal next character to *c* (default CTRL-V).

style	**style** [*options*] *files*
	
	Analyze the writing style and report the readability grades, sentence structure, sentence type, word usage, and sentence beginnings for one or more *files*.
	
	options
	
	    -a print sentence length and readability index.
	    -e print sentences beginning with an expletive.
	    -l *n* print sentences longer than *n* words.
	    -ml skip lists of non-sentences.
	    -mm override **-ms** with **-mm** macro package.
	    -p print sentences containing a passive verb.
	    -P print parts of speech for all words.
	    -r *n* print sentences with a readability index greater than *n*.

su	**su** [-] [*user*] [-*c command*] Create a shell with the effective user id of another *user*. If no *user* is specified, create a superuser shell. Enter CTRL-D to terminate. *options* **-** go through the entire login sequence. Note that, if present, this option must occur before the specified user name.

-c *command*
>   execute *command* via the shell. If *command* is followed by options or arguments, the entire string should be quoted.

---

sum *files*

Calculate and print a checksum and the number of blocks for the named *files*.

sum

---

symorder *orderlist symbolfile*

Rearrange symbols in *symbolfile* as found in *orderlist*.

symorder

---

sync

Update the super block. **sync** should be called to insure file system integrity before the system is shut down.

sync

---

sysline [*options*]

Periodically display system status information on terminal status line.

options

>   **-b**   beep once on the half-hour and twice at the hour.
>   **-c**   clear status line for 5 seconds before redisplay.
>   **-d**   print status line data in readable format.
>   **-D**   print out current day before time.
>   **-e**   do not print control characters.
>   **-w**   print status on current line of terminal.
>   **-H** *host*
>   print load average on remote *host* (VAX only).
>   **-h**   print host machine's name after the time (VAX only).
>   **-l**   do not print names of users logging in and logging out.
>   **-m**   do no check for mail.

sysline

sysline *continued*	**-p** do not report runnable and suspended processes. **-r** do not display in reverse video. **+n** update every *n* seconds (default = 60). **-q** do not print diagnostic messages. **-i** print process id upon startup. **-s** print short form by left-justifying. **-j** force left-justification.
syslog	**syslog** [*options*] Send a message to the system log file. *options* **-** send the lines from standard input. **-i***name* use *name* as the log identifier. **-p** include the process id in the log entry. **-n** log the message at level *n*.
systat	**systat** [*options*] Display system statistics. *options* **-display** specify type of display. **-n** refresh every *n* intervals.
tabs	**tabs** [*options*] [*term*] Set terminal tab stops on specified terminal *term*. *options* **-n** do not indent left margin.
tail	**tail** [*options*] [*file*] Print the last ten lines of the named *file*. *options* **-f** do not terminate at the end of file. **-r** print lines in reverse order.

+*n* [**lbc**]
      begin at *n*th line (default), block, or charac-
      ter from beginning of file. Print to end of
      file.

-*n* [**lbc**]
      begin at *n*th line (default), block, or charac-
      ter from end of file. Print to end of file.

tail
continued

---

talk *user* [*tty*]

Communicate with another *user*. If a *user* is logged in
more than once use *tty* to specify the terminal line.

talk

---

tar [*key*] [*files*]

Copy and restore multiple *files* to or from tape.

function keys (choose only one)

c   create a new tape.

r   append *files* to tape.

t   print the names of *files* if they are stored on
           the tape. If *filesP are not specified, print
           names of all files.)*

u   add files if not on tape or if modified.

x   extract *files* from tape. (if *files* not speci-
           fied, extract all files).

other keys

b*n*   use *n* for blocking factor (maximum is 20,
           default is 1).

B   force input and output blocking to 20
           blocks per record.

-C*dir* used with **-c** and **-r**, this option changes the
           path to the directory *dir* so that *files* can be
           specified with short pathnames.

f   use *file* as archive (default is **/dev/mt?**).

F[F] exclude all SCCS directories. The second F
           tells **tar** to exclude all **.o**, SCCS, **core**,
           a.out, and **err** files.

h   follow symbolic links.

i   ignore checksum errors.

l   print error messages.

m   do not restore modification times.

tar

☞

---

tar *continued*	**o**	suppress directory information.
	p	restore files to original modes.
	n	select tape drive *n* (0-9, default is 8).
	v	print function letter (*x* for extraction or *a* for archive) and name of files.
	w	wait for confirmation (**y** performs the action).
	X *xfile*	exclude the files or directories listed in *xfile*.

tbl

tbl [*options*] [*files*]

A preprocessor for *nroff* and *troff* that formats tables contained in *files* and enclosed by .TS and .TE requests.

options

  -TX   use only full vertical line motions.

tc

tc *options file*

Simulate phototypesetter output on a Tektronix 4014 terminal.

options

  -p*n*   use page length *n*.
  -s*n*   skip the first *n* pages.
  -t   do not wait for newlines at end of page.

tcopy

tcopy *source* [*destination*]

Copy magnetic tapes. With no *destination* tape specified, print information about the size of record and tape files.

tee

tee [*options*] [*files*]

Duplicate the standard input and send one copy to the standard output and one copy to *files*.

options

  -a   append output to *files*.
  -i   ignore all interrupts.

telnet [*host*[*port*]]   **telnet**

Communicate with another host using the TELNET
protocol. Get a summary of commands with "**?**".

---

test *expression*   **test**
or [*expression*]

Evaluate an *expression* and, if its value is true, return a
zero exit status; otherwise, a non-zero exit status is
returned. In shell scripts, you can use the alternate
form [*expression*]. This command is generally used
with conditional constructs in shell programs. See
Section 2 for more details.

primitives

>   **-d** *file* true if *file* exists and is a directory.
>   **-f** *file* true if *file* exists and is a regular file.
>   **-n** *s1* true if the length of string *s1* is nonzero.
>   **-r** *file* true if *file* exists and is readable.
>   **-s** *file* true if *file* exists and has a size greater than
>   zero.
>   **-t** [*n*] true if the open file whose file descriptor
>   number is *n* (default is 1) is associated with
>   a terminal device.
>   **-w** *file* true if *file* exists and is writable.
>   **-z** *s1* true if the length of string *s1* is zero.
>   *s1* = *s2*
>   true if strings *s1* and *s2* are identical.
>   *s1* != *s2*
>   true if strings *s1* and *s2* are *not* identical.
>   *string* true if *string* is not the null string.
>   *n1 op n2*
>   true if comparison *op* between the integers
>   *n1* and *n2* is true. Any of the comparisons
>   **-eq, -ne, -gt, -ge, -lt,** and **-le** may be used
>   as *op*.

These primitives may be combined with the negation
operator (**!**), binary *and* (**-a**), binary *or* (**-o**), and parentheses.

---

tftp	**tftp** [*host*]
	Transfer files to and from remote machine *host*. You will be prompted interactively for commands. Type **?** for a list of commands.
time	**time** *command* [*arguments*]
	Execute a *command* with optional arguments and print the total elapsed time, execution time, process execution time, and system time of the process.
tip	**tip** [*option*] [*name/num*]
	Establish connection to another machine. Remote machine may be identified by a recognizable *name* if it is defined in the files **/etc/remote** and **/etc/phones**, or by a telephone number.

options

-v	display sets as they are made.
-speed	establish connection at baud rate *speed*.

tip runs as two processes: transmit and receive. Transmit reads from standard input and passes lines to the remote system (except lines beginning with "~"). Receive reads data from the remote system (except lines beginning with "~").

Escape sequences

~^D,	hangup and exit from remote system.
~c [*dir*]	change directory to *dir* on local system.
~!	escape to a shell on local system.
~>	copy file from local to remote system.
~<	copy file from remote to local system.
~p *file* [*target*]	send *file* to remote UNIX host.
~t *file* [*target*]	take *file* from a remote UNIX host.
~|	pipe output from remote command to local process.
~$	pipe output from local command to remote process.

~#	send a BREAK to remote system.	**tip**
~s	set a variable.	*continued*
~^Z	stop **tip** (with job control only).	
~^Y	stop only "local" **tip** process (with job control only).	
~?	print summary of tilde escapes.	

tk [*options*] [*file*]   **tk**

Format output for a Tektronix 4014 terminal.

options

-t   do not wait between pages.

-*n*   divide screen into *n* columns and wait after the last column.

-p*n*   set page length to *n* lines.

tn3270 [*system*]   **tn3270**

Establish connection between a UNIX machine and an IBM machine running *VM/CMS*, as if user were on an IBM 3270 terminal. If *system* is not specified, you will be prompted **tn3270>**. You can issue any of the commands **open, close, quit, Z** (to suspend), **status,** or **?** (to print help information).

touch [*options*] [*date*] *files*   **touch**

Update the access and modification time and date to the current time, or the optional *date*, for one or more *files*.

options

-a   update only the access time.

-c   do not create non-existent files.

-f   force **touch** despite read and write permissions.

-m   update only the modification time.

date

The date and time, in the format: *mmddhhmm*[*yy*].

tp	**tp** [*key*] [*name*]

Save and restore files on DECtape or magtape.

function key (choose one)

r named files are written on the tape.

u update the tape only if modification time is later than that on tape (default).

d delete named files from the tape (DECtape only).

x restore named files (or all, if none are named) from the tape.

t list the names of specified files (or all files on the tape, if none are named).

keys

m specify magtape, not DECtape.

n tape is mounted on drive *n*, $0 \leq n \leq 7$. For magtape, 0 is the default.

v verbose: type name of file being processed and the function key.

c clear contents of tape before beginning.

i do not quit when errors are encountered.

f use first named file as the archive, not the tape.

w prompt before treating each file.

---

tr

tr [*options*] [*string1* [*string2*]]

Substitute characters found in *string1* into *string2*.

options

-c complement characters in *string1* with ASCII 001-377.

-d delete characters in *string1* from output.

-s squeeze repeated output characters in *string2*.

---

troff

troff [*options*] [*files*]

Format *files* for printing on a phototypesetter. For more information on **troff**, see Section 5.

---

options

troff
continued

-a   use printable ASCII approximation.

-b   report phototypesetter status.

-f   do not feed out paper at end of run.

-F_dir_ search _dir_ for font width tables instead of default **/usr/lib/font**.

-i   read standard input after files.

-m_name_

      prepend **/usr/lib/tmac/tmac.**_name_ to files.

-n_n_   number first page _n_.

-o_list_ print only pages contained in _list_. A page range is specified by _n-m_.

-p_n_   print all characters in point size _n_.

-q   do not echo .rd requests.

-r_an_ assign _n_ to register _a_.

-s_n_   stop every _n_ pages.

-t   send output to standard output.

-w   if the phototypesetter is busy, wait until it is free.

---

true *options*

true

Return a successful exit status. See also **false**.

---

tset [*options*] [*type*]

tset

Set terminal modes. Without arguments, the terminal is reinitialized according to the TERM environment variable.

options

-   print name of terminal determined upon on standard output.

-e _c_   set erase character to _c_ (default is backspace ^H).

-i_c_   set interrupt character to _c_ (default is ^C).

-I   do not output terminal initialization setting.

-k _c_   set line kill character to _c_ (default is ^X).

-m [*port*][*baudrate*]:*tty*]

      declare terminal specifications.

-n   initialize new tty driver modes (for Berkeley 4BSD driver) for this terminal.

---

tset *continued*	**-Q** do not print "Erase set to" and "Kill set to" messages. **-s** output TERM and TERMCAP assignments in environment. **-S** output TERM and TERMCAP assignments in *csh* environment. *port* the port type (usually **dialup** or **plugboard**). *baudrate* the speed, may be preceded with: >, =, <, @, and !. *tty* terminal type.
tsort	**tsort** [*file*] Perform a topological sort on a *file*.

tty	**tty** [*options*]
	
	 Print the device name of your terminal.
	 options
	    -l print the synchronous line number.
	    -s return only the codes:
	        0 = a terminal.
	        1 = not a terminal.

ul	**ul** [*options*] [*files*]
	
	 Perform underlining on one or more named *files* as specified in the environment variable TERM. If the terminal does not have underlining capabilities, underlining is ignored.
	 options
	    -i show underline one line below text.
	    -t *tty* override TERM variable with terminal type *tty*.

umount	**umount** *options* See the *mount* command.

unifdef [*options*] [*files*]   **unifdef**

Remove *ifdef* lines from a file.

options

   -t   process text not coded in C.

   -l   replace removed lines with blank lines.

   -c   reverse the operation of **unifdef**.

   -D*symbol*

          define *symbol*.

   -U*symbol*

          undefine *symbol*.

   -id*symbol*

          define *symbol* to be ignored but copied out.

   -iu*symbol*

          undefine *symbol* to be ignored but copied
          out.

---

uncompact *file*   **uncompact**

Restore the original *file* compressed by **compact**.

---

uncompress [*options*] [*files*]   **uncompress**

Restore the original file compressed by **compress**.

options

   -f   uncompress unconditionally, i.e. do not
          prompt before overwriting files.

   -v   print the resulting percentage of reduction
          for each compressed file.

   -c   write to the standard output: do not change
          files.

---

unexpand [*options*] [*files*]   **unexpand**

Change blank spaces back to tabs in the named *files*.
See also **expand**.

options

   -a   insert a tab if two or more blank spaces
          occur.

---

unget	**unget** [*options*] *files*
	Restore a previous **get** for one or more SCCS *files*. See also **sccs**; for more information on SCCS, see Section 9.
	options
	-n do not remove file retrieved with **get**.
	-r *sid* the SCCS id version number.
	-s suppress standard output.
uniq	**uniq** [*options*] [*ifile* [*ofile*]]
	Remove duplicate adjacent lines from *ifile* and write the remainder to *ofile*. Often used as a filter.
	options
	-c print unique lines and count repeated lines.
	-d print only one copy of repeated lines.
	-u print only unique lines in *ifile*.
	-*n* ignore first n fields of a line.
	+*n* ignore first n characters of a field.
units	**units**
	Interactively supply a formula to convert a number from one unit to another. The file **/usr/lib/units** gives a complete list of the units. Use ^D to exit.
uptime	**uptime**
	Print the current time, amount of time logged in, number of users logged in, and the system load averages.
users	**users**
	List the currently logged-in users.
uuclean	**uuclean** [*options*]
	Remove files whose name begins with *pre* and older than *time* hours from the *uucp* spool directory.

options

   -m   notify the owner when the specified file is deleted.

   -n *time*

       delete the files older than *time* hours.

   -p *pre* remove files with the prefix *pre*.

uuclean
continued

---

uucp [*options*] [*source!*]*file* [*destination!*]*file*

Copy a file (or group of files) from *source* to *destination*. *source* and *destination* may both be remote systems. The destination file can be a directory.

options

   -a   do not use **getwd** to find current directory.

   -c   do not copy files to the spool directory.

   -C   copy files to the spool directory.

   -d   make directories for the copy when they do not exist (default).

   -f   do not make directories, when they do not exist.

   -m   send mail to user when copy is completed.

   -r   queue job; do not start the transfer.

   -n *user*

       send *user* mail that files were sent.

   -g *x* set priority of job by *c*: the lower *c* is in the ASCII sequence, the earlier it will be transmitted (default = **n**).

   -s *dir* use *dir* as the spool directory.

   -x *level*

       turn off debug mode at specified *level*.

uucp

---

uudecode [*file*]

Read a uuencoded file and recreate the original file with the same mode and name (see **uuencode**).

uudecode

---

uuencode [*file*] *name* | **mail** *remotesys!usr*

Convert a binary *file* to a form which can be sent via mail. The encoding uses only printing ASCII characters, and includes the mode of the file and the *name* the file will be given on the remote system when it is **uudecoded** for recreation on the remote system.

uuencode

☞

uuencode *continued*	Oftne, there is a special *decode* user on the remote system, who automatically **uudecodes** the file. Note that **uuencode** can take standard input, so a single argument will be taken as the name to be given to the file when it is decoded.

uulog	**uulog** [*options*]
	
	Print information from the **uucp** log file.
	options
	    -ssystem
	        print information about work involving *system*.
	    -uuser
	        print commands initiated by *user*.

uuname	**uuname** [*options*] Print the names of systems *uucp* knows about. *options* **-l** print node name of local system.

uuq	**uuq** [*options*]
	
	Examine entries in the UUCP queue.
	options
	    -h print only summary lines for each system.
	    -l long format listing.
	    -ssys output only jobs for systems whose names begin with *sys*.
	    -uuser
	        output only jobs for users whose login names begin with *user*.
	    -djobn
	        delete job number *jobn* from the UUCP queue.
	    -rdir look for files in *dir* instead of default spooling directory.
	    -bbaud
	        compute transfer time using baud rate *baud* instead of default 1200.

uusend [*options*] *file sys1!sys2!* . . . !*remotefile*   **uusend**

uusend sends a file to a location on a remote system.
The system need not be directly connected to the local
system, but a chain of **uucp** links needs to connect the
two systems. All intervening systems must also support **uusend.**

options

-**m** *mode*
> The *mode* of the file on the remote system
> will be the octal value of *mode*.

---

uux [*options*] [*sys!*] *command*]   **uux**

Gather files from various systems and execute a *command* on the specified machine, *sys*.

options

-          use standard input.
-**c**   do not copy local file to the spool directory
           for transfer.
-**C**   force the copy of local files to spool direc-
           tory for transfer.
-**l**   make a link from the original file to the
           spool directory.
-**L**   start up **uucico.**
-**n**   inhibit *mail* notification.
-**p**   use standard input.
-**r**   queue the job but do not start communica-
           tion program (**uucico**).
-**z**   notify the user if the job fails.
-**a** *user*
           use *user* as the user identification.
-**g***c*   set priority of job by *c*: the lower *c* is in the
           ASCII sequence, the earlier it will be trans-
           mitted (default = n).
-**x***num*
           num, 0-9 is the level of debugging output
           desired. High numbers give more output.

---

vacation [*options*]   **vacation**

Return a message to sender announcing that you are
on vacation.

☞

---

vacation
continued
	options
	
	   -**I** initialize the .**vacation.pag** and .**vaca-**
	          tion.dir files.
	  user forward messages to you and send one to
	          the sender.

---

val

val [*options*] *files*

Validate one or more SCCS *files*. See also **sccs**; for more information on SCCS, see Section 9.

options

-**m** *value*
  compare *value* with %M% keyword.
-**r***sid*   the SCCS id version number.
-**s**   suppress standard output.
-**y** *value*
  compare *value* with %Y% keyword.

---

vgrind

vgrind [*options*] *files*

Format program sources using **troff**.

options

-**f**   filter mode.
-   take input from standard input.
-**t**   send formatted text to standard output.
-**n**   do not bold keyword.
-**x**   produce index with special format.
-**W**   output to Versatec printer rather than Varian.
-**s***n*   use point size *n* on output.
-**h** *header*
  place *header* on each output page (default is the filename).
-**d***file*   take language definitions from *file* (default is **/usr/lib/vgrindefs**).
-**l***lang*   use specified language *lang*.

---

vi

vi [*options*] *files*

A screen-oriented text editor based on **ex**. See Section 4 for a summary of commands.

---

options

vi
continued

   -r   retrieve last saved version of *file* after crash.

   -R   read-only mode.

   -t *tag* begin editing named *file* at location *tag*.

   -w*n*   set default window size to *n*.

   -x   edit an encrypted file.

   +[*n*][*pattern*]

         position cursor at end of file, line number *n*, or *pattern*. View the file with **vi** commands but do not make changes.

   -r*file* retrieve last saved version of named *file* after crash.

   -t *tag* begin editing named *file* at location *tag*.

   -w*n*   set default window size to *n*.

   +[*n*][*pattern*]

         position cursor at end of file, line number *n*, or *pattern*.

---

vlp [*options*] *files*

vlp

Format files to be run through **nroff**, **vtroff** or **troff**.

options

   -p*n*   change pointsize to *n* (default = 8).

   -d   debug mode.

   -f   filter mode.

   -l   do not place labels next to functions.

   -v   send output to **vtroff** instead of standard output.

   -T*title*print *title* on each page of output. This option may be specified for each file.

---

vmstat [*options*] [*drives*] [*interval* [*n*]]

vmstat

Report *cpu* activity *n* times every *interval* seconds.

options

   -f   report only on **forks** and **vforks**.

   -s   print contents of the **sum** structure.

   -i   report on number of interrupts taken by each device.

---

vnews	**vnews** [*options*]
	
	Read news articles posted over the Usenet.
	options
	    -a*date*
	          select articles posted after *date*.
	    -n*groups*
	          select articles belonging to *groups*.
	    -t*strings*
	          select titles containing one of the listed *strings*.
	    -r print articles in reverse order.
	    -x select articles that have already been read as well as new ones.
	    -u update **.newsrc** file every 5 minutes.
	    -c print first page of each article.
	    -s print newsgroup subscription list.

vwidth	**vwidth** *fontfile pointsize* **> ft.xx.c** Translate width information from **vfont** style format to **troff** format.

w	**w** [*options*] [*user*]
	
	Print who is on the system and what they are doing.
	options
	    -h suppress the heading.
	    -l long form of output.
	    -s short form of output.

wait	**wait** Wait for all background processes to complete and report their termination status. If n is specified, wait only for the process with process id n. Used in shell scripts.
wall	**wall** *message* Send a message to all users. End message with ^D.

wc [*options*] *files*
 	
Print a character, word, and line count for *files*.
options
   -c   character count only.
   -l   line count only.
   -w   word count only.
	wc

what *files* Print which versions of object modules were used to construct a file.	**what**
whatis *commands* Give a short description of one or more *commands*.	**whatis**

whereis [*options*] [*diroptions*] *files*
 	
Locate source, binary, or manual sections for one or more *files*.
options
   -b   search for binary files.
   -m   search for manual sections.
   -s   search for source files.
   -u   search for unusual entries.
diroptions
   -f   terminate directory list.
   -B   search binary files.
   -M   search manual sections.
   -S   search source files.
	whereis

which [*commands*] List the files which would be executed had *commands* been given as commands.	**which**
who [*file*] List the names of users currently logged onto the system, or your current login name. Specify *file* for a file other than **/etc/utmp** to be examined.	**who**

whoami	**whoami** Print the user name you are logged in as.
whois	**whois** *name* Print information about a specific user.

window	**window** [*options*]
	
	Implement a window environment on ASCII terminals.
	options
	    -t terse mode.
	    -f fast: do not perform startup action.
	    -d create the two default windows.
	    -e *c* set escape character to *c*.
	    -c *command*
	            execute *command* before proceeding.

write	**write** *user* [*tty*] *message* Initiate or respond to an interactive conversation with *user*. A write session is terminated with ^D. *tty* the *tty* number if the user is logged on to more than one terminal.
xget	**xget** Receive secure mail. This command prompts for your *password*. See also **enroll** and **xsend**.
xsend	**xsend** *user* Send secure mail to *user*. See also **enroll** and **xget**.
xstr	**xstr** [*options*] [*file*] Extract strings from a C source *file* to implement shared strings.

options

   -   read standard input.

   -c*name*

         extract strings from *name*.

   -v   verbose mode.

xstr
continued

---

yacc [*options*] *file*

Yet another compiler-compiler.

options

   -d   generate **y.tab.h** with define statements.

   -v   produce **y.output**.

yacc

---

yes [*expletive*]

Repeatedly output **y** (yes) or an optional *expletive*.

yes

---

zcat [*files*]

Uncompress a file to the standard output. See **compress**.

zcat

Shell

2

Shell Syntax

- **The C Shell**
- **The Bourne Shell**

   The following subsections are provided for each shell:

   - Special Files
   - Filename Metacharacters
   - Variable Substitution
   - Special Symbols
   - Shell Variables
   - Built-in Commands

- **Comparison of Bourne and C Shells**

The C Shell

Note: The C-shell is not officially part of UNIX System V; however, it is included in one form or another on many systems.

Special Files

~/.cshrc	executed at each instance of shell
~/.login	executed by login shell after .cshrc at login
~/.logout	executed by login shell at logout
/etc/passwd	source of home directories for ~name abbreviations

Filename Metacharacters

*	match any string of zero or more characters
?	match any single character
[...]	match any of the enclosed characters. A pair of characters separated by a dash will match any character lexically between the pair.
{abc, xxx, ... }	match each comma-separated string enclosed in braces; e.g., ls {ch, sec}? might yield ch1 ch2 sec1 sec2.
~	home directory for the current user
~name	substitute home directory of user name

Variable Substitution

In the following substitutions, braces ({ }) can be used to separate a variable name from following characters that would otherwise be a part of it.

$variable ${variable}	use value of variable
$name [n] ${name [n]}	select word number n from name
$#name ${#name}	return the number of words in name
$1 ... $9 ${1} ... ${9}	arguments on command line
$*	all arguments on command line: "$1 ... $9"

The variable substitutions above may be followed by one **modifier** from the set:

:g, :h, :r, :t, :x, :gh, :gr, :gt

Modifiers are described more fully later in this section.

$?name ${?name}	return 1 if *name* is set; 0 if *name* is not set
$$	process number of parent shell
$<	read a line from standard input

Special Symbols

|	perform pipeline (use output of preceding command as input of following command, e.g., **cat** *file* | **lpr**)
;	separate sequential commands on same line
&	run command in background (e.g., **lpr** *file*&)
&&	execute command if previous command was successful (e.g., **grep** *string file* && **lpr** *file*)
||	execute command if previous command was unsuccessful (e.g., **grep** *string1 file* || **grep** *string2 file*)
'...'	take all characters between single quotation marks literally. (Don't allow special character meaning.)
\	take following character literally
"..."	take enclosed characters literally but allow variable and command substitution
`cmd`	use output of *cmd* as an argument to another command
>!*file*	*redirect to file even when* **noclobber** *is set*
|&	pipe standard error along with standard output
#	begin a comment in a shell file
<*file*	take input from *file*
<<*string*	read standard input up to a line identical to *string*
>*file*	redirect output to *file*
>>*file*	redirect output to end of *file*
>&*file*	redirect both standard output and standard error to *file*

Shell

argv	contains shell argument list of current command
cdpath	can be set to list of directories searched to find a subdirectory if the subdirectory is not in current directory; e.g. "**set cdpath** = (/usr/lib); cd **macros**" is equivalent to "**cd /usr/lib/macros**"
cwd	contains full pathname of current directory
echo	if set, specify each command and argument before execution
histchars	characters to be used by history mechanism
history	can be set to the numeric value for size of history list, e.g. "**set history = 25**"
home	contains the home directory of user
ignoreeof	if set, ignore end-of-file from terminals. This prevents the shell from accidentally being logged out
mail	can be set to specify the file where the shell checks for mail, e.g. "**set mail = /usr/spool/mail/tim**"
noclobber	if set, restrict output redirection to prevent accidental destruction of files
noglob	if set, inhibit filename expansion
nonomatch	if set, it is not an error for filename expansion not to match any existing files
notify	if set, notify size of process completions as they occur; otherwise, notify only when the current job is completed
path	can be set to specify the search path for commands, e.g. "**set path = (. /usr/bin)**"
prompt	the string that is printed before each command is read from interactive input (default is %.) Can be set to reflect current event number from the history list, e.g. "**set prompt = 'tom \!%'.**"
shell	contains the pathname of the shell currently being used
status	contains return status of last command. a value of 0 = normal exit, a value of 1 = command failed.
time	can be set to control automatic timing of commands. If command takes more than $time cpu seconds to execute, then the utilization time is printed for the command; e.g. "**set time = 3.**"
verbose	if set, the words of each command will be printed after history substitution.

Expression Operators

Operators are listed in descending order of precedence.

-, +	unary minus and plus
~	binary inversion
!	logical negation
*, /, %	multiplication, division, modulus
+, -	addition, subtraction
<<, >>	left shift, right shift
<=	less than or equal to
>=	greater than or equal to
<	less than
>	greater than
==	equality (left to right)
!=	inequality
=~	equality in which right hand side is a pattern containing *, ? or [...]
!~	inequality in which right hand side is a pattern containing *, ? or [...]
&	binary AND
^	binary exclusive OR
|	binary OR
&&	logical AND
||	logical OR
()	parenthesized expression for grouping. Necessary if the expression contains <, >, &, or |.
{cmd}	1 if *cmd* terminates with 0 exit status; 0 otherwise.

Expression operators may also include logical file enquiries of the form *-l name* where *l* is one of:

d	directory
e	existence
f	plain file
o	ownership
r	read access
w	write access
x	execute access
z	zero size

and *name* is command and filename expanded before the test is performed.

History Event Selection

!!	re-execute last command
!*n*	re-execute command *n* from history list
!*pattern*	re-execute most recent command from the history list that begins with *pattern*
!?*pattern*?	re-execute most recent command from the history list that contains *pattern*

Word Specifications

Within history substitutions it is possible to select individual words in the command to supply or to modify the previous command. Follow event by a colon ":" to access the following words except where it is stated that the colon may be omitted.

0	first word (command name) e.g. **!!:0**
n	(*n*+1)th word e.g. **!!:3**
^	second word (first argument) (colon may be omitted) e.g. **!!^**
$	last word (colon may be omitted) e.g. **!!$**
%	match the word of the immediately preceding ?*pattern*? (colon may be omitted)
x-y	range of arguments from *x* through *y* e.g. **!!:5-7**
-y	abbreviates '0-y' (colon may be omitted)
*****	stands for ^$ (colon may be omitted)
*x***	abbreviate *x*–$ where *x* is position number
x-	like *x** but omitting last word

History Modifiers

Follow event or **optional** word designations with a modifier below to perform the following functions:

:e	remove all but the extension **.xxx** e.g. **!!:3:e**
:h	remove trailing pathname leaving the head e.g. **!!$:h**
:p	command is printed but not executed e.g. **!!*:p**
:r	remove trailing **.xxx** leaving root name e.g. **!!$:r**
:s/*old***/***new*	substitute new contents for old contents e.g. **!!:s/tim/jim/** To substitute string in immediately preceding command, you may use **^**, e.g. **!!:s/tim/jim/ = ^tim^jim.**
:q	quote the substituted values and prevent further substitutions e.g. **!!:s/jim/sim/:q**
:t	remove leading pathname leaving tail e.g. **!!:3:t**
:x	divide words at blanks, tabs, and newlines e.g. **!!:x**
:&	repeat previous substitution e.g. **!6:&**
:g	change globally e.g. **!!:g:s/tim/jim/**

alias [*name*] [*cmd*]   **alias**

Assign *name* as the alias for *cmd*. If *cmd* is not
specified, print the alias for *name*; if *name* also is not
specified, print all aliases.

---

bg [*%job* ...]   **bg**

Put the current or the specified jobs into background.
Same as *%jobn* **&**.

---

break   **break**

Resume execution after end of nearest enclosing
while or **foreach**.

---

breaksw   **breaksw**

Cause break from a switch: continue execution after
endsw.

---

case *pattern*   **case**

Identify a *pattern* in a **switch**.

---

cd [*dir*]   **cd**

Change working directory to *dir*; default is home
directory of user.

chdir	**chdir** [*dir*]
	Same as **cd**.
continue	**continue**
	Continue execution of nearest enclosing **while** or **foreach**.
default	**default**
	Label the default case in a **switch**.
dirs	**dirs**
	Print the directory stack.
echo	**echo** [**-n**] *string*
	Write *string* to standard output; if **-n** is specified, the output is not terminated by a newline.
eval	**eval** *arg* ...
	Evaluate arguments as a command line and use the result as input to the shell.
exec	**exec** *command*
	Execute *command* in place of current shell.

exit [(*expr*)]

Exit shell with status value of last command or value
specified by *expr*.

exit

---

fg [%*job*...]

Bring current or specified job to the foreground.
Same as %*jobn*.

fg

---

foreach *name* (*wordlist*)
    commands
end

Set variable name to each member of *wordlist* and
execute *commands* between **foreach** and **end**.

foreach

---

glob *wordlist*

Like **echo**, but no "\" escapes are recognized, and
words are delimited by null characters.

glob

---

goto *string*

Continue execution following the next occurrence of
string followed by a :, which may be preceded by
blanks and tabs but otherwise must be alone on the
line.

goto

---

hashstat

Print the statistics for the effectiveness of the internal
hash table used for locating commands in path.

hashstat

Shell

history	**history** Display the list of history events. (History syntax is discussed earlier in this section.)

if	**if** (*expression*) *command*
	    or **if** (*expr1*) **then**
	        commands1
	    [**else if** (*expr2*) **then**
	        commands2]
	        ⋮
	    else
	        commands3
	    endif
	
	If *expression* is true, do *command*.
	
	Or if *expr1* is true, then execute *commands1*; else if *expr2* is true, then execute *commands2*; if neither is true, execute *commands3*.

jobs	**jobs** [-l] List of active jobs; if -l is specified, process ids are printed as well.
kill	**kill** [-*sig*] *pid* Terminate the designated process (*pid*) optionally with a signal (*sig*). **kill** -l will list available signal names.
limit	**limit** *resource maximum-use* Limit the consumption by the current process and each process it creates to not individually exceed *maximum-use* on the specified *resource*. If no *maximum-use* is given, then the current limit is printed; if no *resource* is given, then all limitations are

given. Resources include **cputime, filesize, datasize, stacksize,** and **coredumpsize.**	**limit** *continued*

login Replace login shell with **/bin/login.**	**login**

logout Terminate login shell.	**logout**

newgrp *group* Change the group id of the caller. A new shell is executed and the current shell state is lost.	**newgrp**

nice [*+number*] command Schedule a command to be performed at a low priority where *number* is the priority number and *command* is the command to be performed; default number is 4.	**nice**

nohup [*command*] Do not terminate command if terminal line is closed. Use without command in shell scripts to keep script from being terminated.	**nohup**

notify [*%job* ...] Causes shell to report a change of status for the current or specified jobs.	**notify**

onintr	**onintr** [-] [*label*] Restore the default action of shell on interrupts. With the - option, ignore all interrupts; with *label*, cause the shell to execute a "**goto** *label*" when an interrupt is received.
popd	**popd** +*n* Pop the directory stack and return to the new top directory; +*n* discards the *n*th entry in the stack.
pushd	**pushd** [*name*] or **pushd** +*n* Change to *name* directory and add current directory to the stack. With no *name* specified, exchange the top two elements of the directory stack. Or change to *n*th directory and put it on top of the stack.
rehash	**rehash** Recompute hash table for *path*. Use whenever a new command is added to path during the current session.
rcpeat	**repeat** *n command* Execute *n* instances of *command*.
set	**set** [*variable* [*n*] [=*value* . . .]] Set *variable* to *value*, or if multiple values are specified, set the variable to the list of words in the value list. If an index *n* is specified, set the *n*th word in the variable to *value*. (The variable must already

contain at least that number of words.) With no arguments, display value of all set variables.	**set** *continued*
setenv *name value* Set the value of *name* to be *value* (a single string). **setenv** is not necessary for the **USER, TERM** and **PATH** variables.	**setenv**
shift [*array*] Shift positional arguments in specified *array*; e.g. **$2** becomes **$1**.	**shift**
source *file* Read commands from *file*.	**source**
stop [*%job . . .*] Stop the current or specified job executing in background.	**stop**
suspend Stop the shell, as if it were sent a **stop** signal with $$.	**suspend**

switch *(string)*
case *pattern1*:
    commands
[**breaksw**]
case *pattern2*:
    commands
     ⋮
	switch
	
	☞

switch *continued*	[breaksw] **default:** *commands* [breaksw] **endsw** Match each case *pattern* against the specified *string*. Execute commands following each pattern that matches, or after **default:** if no pattern matches. Use **breaksw** to break out of the switch once a match has been made.
time	**time** [*command*] Display a summary of time used by *command* or by the shell if no arguments are specified.
umask	**umask** [*nnn*] Display file creation mask or set file creation mask to octal *nnn*. The file creation mask determines which permission bits are turned off; e.g., **umask 002** produces **rw-rw-r--**.
unalias	**unalias** *name* Remove *name* from the alias list. See **alias**.
unhash	**unhash** Remove internal hash table.
unlimit	**unlimit** [*resource*] Remove the limitations on *resource*. If *resource* is not specified, remove limitations on all resources. See **limit**.

unset *pattern*

Remove variables that match specified *pattern* (filename metacharacters may be used in *pattern*).

---

unsetenv *name*

Remove environment variables that match specified *name* (filename metacharacters may be used in *name*).

---

wait

Wait for all background jobs to terminate.

---

while *(expression)* ...
    commands
end

While the *expression* evaluates non-zero, evaluate *commands* between **while** and **end**. **break** and **continue** can be used to terminate or continue the loop.

@ [*variable* [*n*] = *expression*]

Assign the value of the arithmetic *expression* to *variable*, or to the *n*th element of *variable* if the index *n* is specified. Expression operators are listed earlier in this section. With no variable or expression specified, print the values of all shell variables. The special formats **@** *variable*++ and **@** *variable*-- will increment and decrement *variable* by one, respectively.

The Bourne Shell

Special Files

$HOME/.profile   executed automatically at login

Filename Metacharacters

*	match any string of zero or more characters
?	match any single character
[abc ...]	match any one of the enclosed characters. A pair of characters separated by a dash will match any character lexically between the pair.
![abc ...]	match any character *not* enclosed as above

Variable Substitution

variable=value ...	set *variable* to *value*
$*variable*	use value of *variable*
$*variable*[:]-*value*	use *variable* if set; otherwise set to *value*
$*variable*[:]=*value*	use *variable* if set; otherwise set to *value* and assign *value* to *variable*
$*variable*[:]?*value*	use *variable* if set; otherwise print *value*, then exit
$*variable*[:]+*value*	use *value* if *variable* is set; otherwise nothing

If the colon (:) is included in the above expressions then a test is performed to see if the variable is non-null as well as set. Note that there should be no spaces used in the above expressions.

Shell Variables

The following variables are automatically set by the shell. (Note that the $ is not actually part of the variable name. Any of the substitution patterns shown above can be used.)

$#	number of command line arguments
$-	options supplied in invocation or by the set command
$?	exit value of last executed command
$$	exit process number of current process
$!	exit process number of last background command
$1 ... $9	arguments on command line
$*	all arguments on command line ("$1 $2 ... ")
$@	all arguments on command line, individually quoted ("$1" "$2" ...)

The following variables are used by the shell but are not automatically set.

CDPATH	directories searched by **cd**
HOME	home directory defined in **passwd** file
IFS	internal field separators; default space, tab and newline
MAIL	default mail file
MAILCHECK	number of seconds between periodic mail checks
MAILPATH	files checked for mail, delimited by colon
PATH	search path for commands (default is **:/bin:/usr/bin**)
PS1	primary prompt string; default is **$**
PS2	secondary prompt string; default is **>**
SHACCT	file to write accounting information
SHELL	name of the shell
TERM	terminal type

Special Symbols

|	perform pipeline (use output of preceding command as input of following command, e.g., **cat** *file* | **lpr**)
;	separate sequential commands on same line
&	run command in background (e.g., **lpr** *file***&**)
&&	execute command if previous command was successful (e.g., **grep** *string file* **&& lpr** *file*)
||	execute command if previous command was unsuccessful (e.g., **grep** *string1 file* || **grep** *string2 file*)
( )	execute commands enclosed in ( ) in a subshell; output from the entire set can then be redirected as a unit or placed in the background. Commands should be separated by ; within the parens.
{ }	execute commands enclosed in { } in current shell
name ( ) {*cmds*}	define function *name*
´...´	take all characters between single quotation marks literally; don't allow special character meaning.
\	take following character literally
"..."	take enclosed characters literally but allow variable and command substitution
`cmd`	use output of *cmd* as argument to another command
#	begin a comment in a shell file
<*file*	take input from *file*
<<*string*	read standard input up to a line identical to *string*
>*file*	redirect output to *file* (overwrite)
>>*file*	redirect output to end of *file* (append)
<&*n*	duplicate standard input from *n* e.g. 2<&3
<&–	close standard input
n>	redirect output from *n* instead of default 1
n<	redirect input from *n* instead of default 0

Built-In Bourne Shell Commands

:	**:** Null command. Returns an exit status of 0.
.	**.** *file* Read and execute indicated *file*. *file* does not have to be executable.
break	**break** [*n*] Exit from a **for** or **while** for the *n* innermost levels.

case	**case** *value* **in**
	    pattern [|*pattern*]) *cmd*;;
	        :
	    pattern [|*pattern*]) *cmd*;;
	esac
	
	Execute each *cmd* for which *value* matches the specified *pattern*. If a second pattern is specified (preceded by a |), execute *cmd* if *value* matches either pattern. Patterns can use file generation metacharacters.

cd	**cd** [*dir*] Change working directory to *dir*; default is home directory of user.
continue	**continue** [*n*] Resume *n*-th enclosing **for** or **while** loop.

echo *string*   **echo**

Write *string* to standard output. The following **echo**
escape characters have special meaning in the Bourne
shell:

\b	backspace
\c	suppress terminating newline
\f	formfeed
\n	newline
\r	carriage return
\t	tab character
****	backslash
\nnn	character with ASCII value *nnn*, *nnn* an octal number of 1 to 3 digits beginning with 0.

These escapes must be quoted so they are not interpreted directly by the shell.

---

eval [*args*]   **eval**

Evaluate *args* as a command line and use the result
as input to the shell.

---

exec [*command*]   **exec**

Execute *command* in place of current shell.

---

exit [*n*]   **exit**

Exit the shell with exit status *n*, e.g. **exit 1**. If *n* is
not given, exit status will be that of last command
given.

---

export [*variable* ...]   **export**

Export *variable* to environment of subsequently executed commands. If no argument is given, the list of
exportable variables is printed.

---

for	**for** *variable* [**in** *list*] **do** *commands* **done** For variable *x* (in optional *list* of values) do *commands*. If *list* is omitted, $@ is assumed.
hash	**hash** [**-r**] [*commands*] Search for *commands* and note where they are located, or if *commands* are not specified, list current hashed commands. The -r option will remove *commands* from the hash list.

if	**if** *condition1*
	then *commands1*
	[**elif** *condition2*
	    then *commands2*]
	       ⋮
	[**else** *commands3*]
	fi
	
	If *condition1* is met, do *commands1*; else if *condition2* is met, do *commands2*; if neither is met, do *commands3*. Conditions are usually specified with the **test** command.

login	**login** [*user*] Log in as another user.
newgrp	**newgrp** [*group*] Change the group id of the caller.

pwd Print the present working directory to standard output.	**pwd**
read *variable1* [*variable2* ...] Read one line of standard input, and assign each word to the corresponding *variable*, with all leftover words assigned to last variable. If only one variable is specified, the entire line will be assigned to that variable.	**read**
readonly [*variable1* *variable2* ...] Specify *variables* as read only, or list current read only variables.	**readonly**
return [*n*] Stop execution of function with exit status *n*, or with exit status of previously executed command.	**return**
set [*options*[[--] *arg* ...]] With no arguments **set** prints the values of all variables known to the current shell. The following options can be enabled (-option) or disabled (+option). Specifying -- before listing arguments will prevent those beginning with - from being interpreted as options. **a** Automatically export all subsequently defined variables **e** Exit in bad status if non-interactive **f** Disable file name generation **h** Remember location of commands used in functions as they are defined	**set**

☞

Shell

set *continued*	**k** Put keywords in an environment for a command **n** Read but do not execute commands **t** Exit after one command is executed **u** Treat unset variables as an error **v** Print input lines as they are read **x** Print commands when executed *arg* ... Assigned in order to **$1, $2,** ...
shift	**shift** [*n*] Shift positional arguments; e.g. **$2** becomes **$1**. If *n* is specified, shift to the left *n* places.

test	**test** *expression* [I *expression*]
	or [*expression*]
	
	Evaluate an *expression* and, if its value is true, return a zero exit status; otherwise, return a non-zero exit status. An alternate form of the command uses "[ ]" rather than the word *test*.
	The following primitives are used to construct *expression*.
	
	    -b *file* true if *file* exists and is a block special file
	    -c *file* true if *file* exists and is a character special file
	    -d *file* true if *file* exists and is a directory
	    -f *file* true if *file* exists and is a regular file
	    -g *file* true if *file* exists and its set-group-id bit is set
	    -k *file* true if *file* exists and its sticky bit is set
	    -n *string*
	        true if the length of *string* is non-zero
	    -p *file* true if *file* exists and is a named pipe (fifo)
	    -r *file* true if *file* exists and is readable
	    -s *file* true if *file* exists and has a size greater than zero
	    -t [*n*] true if the open file whose file descriptor number is *n* (default is 1) is associated with a terminal device

-u *file* true if *file* exists and its set-user-id bit is
set
-w *file*
true if *file* exists and is writable
-x *file* true if *file* exists and is executable
-z *s1* true if the length of string *s1* is zero
s1 = *s2*
true if strings *s1* and *s2* are identical
s1 != *s2*
true if strings *s1* and *s2* are *not* identical
string true if *string* is not the null string
n1 op n2
true if comparison *op* between the integers
n1 and *n2* is true. Any of the comparisons
-eq, -ne, -gt, -ge, -lt, and **-le** may be used
as *op*.

These primitives may be combined with the negation
operator (!), binary *and* (**-a**), binary *or* (**-o**), and
parentheses. Operators and operands must be delimited by spaces.

---

times   **times**

Print accumulated process times.

---

trap [[*commands*] *signals*]   **trap**

Execute *commands* if any of *signals* is received.
Multiple commands should be quoted as a group and
separated by semicolons internally. If *commands* is
the null string (i.e., **trap ""** *signals*), then *signals*
will be ignored by the shell. If *commands* are omitted entirely, reset processing of specified signals to
the default action. If both *commands* and *signals* are
omitted, list current trap assignments. Signals are as
follows:

0   exit from shell
1   hangup
2   interrupt
3   quit
4   illegal instruction

☞

---

trap *continued*	**5**	trace trap
	6	IOT instruction
	7	EMT instruction
	8	floating point exception
	10	bus error
	12	bad argument to a system call
	13	write to a pipe without a process to read it
	14	alarm timeout
	15	software termination

type

type *commands*

Print information about specified *commands*.

ulimit

ulimit [*option*] [*n*]

Set the maximum size of files or pipes written by child processes to *n* blocks. Options are **f** (file size, the default) and **p** (pipe size). With no arguments, print the current setting, with **0** signifying no limit.

umask

umask [*nnn*]

Display file creation mask or set file creation mask to octal value *nnn*. The file creation mask determines which permission bits are turned off; e.g., **umask 002** produces **rw-rw-r--**.

unset

unset *names*

Erase definitions of functions or variables listed in *names*.

until

until *condition*
do
          commands
done

Until *condition* is met, do *commands*. *condition* is usually specified with the **test** command.	**until** *continued*
wait [*n*] Wait for process with identification number *n* to terminate and report its status, or for all child processes to finish.	**wait**
while *condition* **do** *commands* **done** While *condition* is met, do *commands*. *Condition* is usually specified with the **test** command.	**while**
filename Read and execute commands from executable file *filename*.	*filename*

The Bourne Shell vs. The C Shell

Syntactic Features
Common to Both Shells

Function	csh	sh
Prompt	%	#
Begin program	#	:
Redirect output	>	>
Force output	>!	
Append to file	>>	>>
Force append	>>!	
Redirect input	<	<
"Here" document	<<	<<
Combine stdout and stderr	>&	2>&1
Read from terminal	$<	read
Pipe output	|	|
Obsolete pipe		^
Run process in background	&	&
Separate commands on same line	;	;
Match any character(s) in filename	*	*
Match single character in filename	?	?
Match any characters enclosed	[ ]	[ ]
Execute in subshell	( )	( )
Match each element in enclosed list	{ }	{ }
Substitute output of enclosed command	` `	` `
Partial quote (allows variable and command expansion)	" "	" "
Full quote	' '	' '
Quote following character	\	\
Begin comment	#	:
Home directory	$home	$HOME
Assign value to variable	set	=
Use value for variable	$var	$var
Process id	$$	$$
Command name	$0	$0
nth argument (0<n<9)	$n	$n
All arguments as a simple "word"	$*	$*
All arguments as separate "words"		$@
Number of arguments	$#argv or $#	$#
Exit status	$status	$?
Background exit status		$!
Current options		$-
Interpret file	source	.

3

Pattern Matching

A number of UNIX text processing programs, including *ed*, *ex*, *vi*, *sed, awk*, and *grep*, allow you to perform searches, and in some cases make changes, by searching for text patterns rather than fixed strings. These text patterns (also called regular expressions) are made up by combining normal characters with a number of special characters.

Metacharacters

The special characters and their use are listed below:

.	Matches any *single* character except *newline*.
*	Matches any number (including zero) of the single character (including a character specified by a regular expression) that immediately precedes it. For example, since "." (dot) means any character, ".*" means "match any number of characters".
[...]	Matches any *one* of the characters enclosed between the brackets. For example, "[AB]" matches either "A" or "B". A range of consecutive characters can be specified by separating the first and last characters in the range with a hyphen. For example, "[A-Z]" will match any upper case letter from "A" to "Z" and "[0-9]" will match any digit from "0" to "9". Some metachararacters lose special meaning inside brackets. A circumflex (^) as the first character in the bracket reverses the sense: it tries to match any one character *not* in the list.
\{*n,m*\}	Matches a range of occurrences of the single character (including a character specified by a regular expression) that immediately precedes it. *n* and *m* are integers between 0 and 256 that specify how many occurrences to match. \{*n*\} will match exactly *n* occurrences, \{*n,*\} will match at least *n* occurrences, and \{*n,m*\} will match any number of occurrences between *n* and *m*. For example, "A\{2,3\}" will match either "AA" (as in "AARDVARK") or "AAA" (as in "AAA Travel Agency") but will not match the single letter "A".
^	Requires that the following regular expression be found at the beginning of the line.
$	Requires that the preceding regular expression be found at the end of the line.
\	Treats the following special character as an ordinary character. For example, "\." stands for a period and "*" for an asterisk.
\(\)	Saves the pattern enclosed between "\(" and "\)" into a special holding space. Up to nine patterns can be saved in this way on a single line. They can be "replayed" in substitutions by the escape sequences "\1" to "\9". Not used in **grep** and **egrep**.
n	Matches the *n*th pattern previously saved by "\(" and "\)", where *n* is a number from 0 to 9 and previously saved patterns are counted from the left on the line. Not used in **grep** and **egrep**.

    &   Prints the entire search pattern when used in a replacement string.

egrep and **awk** use an extended set of metacharacters:

regexp +	Matches one or more occurrences of the regular expression.
regexp ?	Matches 0 or 1 occurrences of the regular expression.
regexp | *regexp*	Matches lines containing either *regexp*.
(*regexp*)	Used for grouping.

ex regular expressions (: commands from **vi**) offer an extended set of metacharacters:

\<	Matches characters at beginning (\<) or at the end (\>) of
\>	a word. The expression "\<ac" would only match words which began with "ac," such as "action" but not "react."
\u	Convert first character of replacement string to uppercase.
\U	Convert replacement string to uppercase.
\l	Convert first character of replacement string to lowercase.
\L	Convert replacement string to lowercase.

Pattern Matching Examples

For example, you can use patterns in the following **vi** and **ex** commands:

/*pattern*	Search for *pattern*.
?*pattern*	Search backwards for *pattern*.
:d/*pattern*/	Deletes from the cursor position up to *pattern*.
:s/*pattern*/*replacement*/	Substitute *replacement* for *pattern*.
:g/*pattern*/*command*	Globally perform *command* on every line containing *pattern*.
:%s/*pattern*/*replacement*/g	Globally substitute *replacement* for *pattern*.
:/*pattern1*/,/*pattern2*/d	Delete the lines between *pattern1* and *pattern2*, inclusive.
:/*pattern1*/,/*pattern2*/co *line*	Copy the lines between *pattern1* and *pattern2*, inclusive, to *line*.
:/*pattern1*/,/*pattern2*/mo *line*	Move the lines between *pattern1* and *pattern2*, inclusive, to *line*.

You can use patterns in the following **sed** commands:

/*pattern*/**a**\ *text*	Insert *text* on the line(s) following *pattern*.
/*pattern*/**i**\ *text*	Insert *text* on the line before *pattern*.
/*pattern*/**c**\ *text*	Change the line addressed by *pattern* to *text*.
s/*pattern*/*replacement*/	Substitute *replacement* for *pattern*.
/*pattern*/**d**	Delete lines containing *pattern*.

UNIX in a Nutshell

4

Editor Command Summary

This section is divided into four major parts:

- The **vi** editor.
- The **ex** editor.
- The **sed** editor.
- The **awk** data manipulation language.

The vi Editor

—Review of vi Operations—

Entering vi

$ vi [+n|+/pattern/] [file]

Open *file* for editing, optionally at line *n* or at the first line matching *pattern*. If no file is specified, open *vi* with an empty buffer. See Section 1 for more information on command-line options for *vi*.

Command Mode

Once the file is opened, you are in command mode. From command mode, you can invoke insert mode, issue editing commands, move the cursor to a different position in the file, invoke *ex* commands or a UNIX shell, and save or exit the current version of the file.

Insert Mode

The following commands invoke insert mode:

   a A i I o O R s S

While in insert mode, you can enter new text in the file. Press the ESCAPE key to exit insert mode and return to command mode.

Command Syntax

The syntax for editing commands is:

   [*n*] *operator* [*m*] *object*

The commands that position the cursor in the file represent objects which the basic editing operators can take as arguments. Objects represent all characters up to (or back to) the designated object. The cursor movement keys and pattern matching commands can be used as objects.

The basic editing operators are:

   c   For change

   d   For delete

   y   For yank or copy

If the current line is the object of the operation, then the operator is the same as the object: **cc, dd, yy.** *n* and *m* are the number of times the operation is performed or the number of objects the operation is performed on. If both *n* and *m* are specified, the effect is *n* × *m*.

The following text objects are represented:

word   Includes characters up to a space or punctuation mark. Capitalized object is variant form which recognizes only blank spaces.

sentence   Is up to . ! ? followed by two spaces.

paragraph   Is up to next blank line or paragraph macro defined by **para=** option.

section   Is up to next section heading defined by **sect=** option.

Examples:

   2cw   Change the next two words
   d}   Delete up to next paragraph
   d^   Delete back to beginning of line
   5yy   Copy the next five lines
   3dl   Delete three characters right of cursor

Status Line Commands

Most commands are not echoed on the screen as you input them. However, the status line at the bottom of the screen is used to echo input for the following commands:

   / ?   For pattern matching search

   :   Invoke an *ex* command

   !   Invoke a UNIX command that takes as its input an object in the buffer and replaces it with output from the command.

Commands that are input on the status line must be entered by pressing the RETURN key. In addition, error messages and output from the ^G command are displayed on the status line.

For more information on *vi*, refer to the Nutshell Handbook, *Learning the vi Editor*.

Saving and Exiting

ZZ	Quit *vi*, saving changes
:wq	Quit *vi*, saving changes
:q!	Force quit and ignore changes
:w	Save changes and stay in file
:w *file*	Save copy to *file*
:f *file*	Change current filename to *file*
:w *%.old*	Use current filename to save as *file.old*
:n1,n2w *file*	Write line *n1* to *n2* to *file*
:w!	Force overwrite of existing file

Editing Multiple Files

:e *file*	Edit another *file*; current file becomes alternate
:e!	Restore last saved version of current file
:e + *file*	Begin editing at end of *file*
:e +n *file*	Open *file* at line *n*
:e #	Open to previous position in alternate file
:ta *tag*	Edit file at location *tag*
:n	Edit next file
:n!	Forces next file
:n *files*	Specify new list of *files*
^G	Show current file and line number
:args	Display multiple files to be edited
:rew	Rewind list of multiple files to top

Inserting New Text

a	Insert after cursor
A	Append to end of line
i	Insert before cursor
I	Insert at beginning of line
o	Insert one line below cursor
O	Insert one line above cursor
ESC	Terminate insert mode
^J	Move down one line
^W	Move back one word
RETURN	Add a newline
BACKSPACE	Move back one character
KILL	Delete current line (set with **stty**)
^H	Move back one character
^I	Insert a tab
^T	Move to next tab setting
^V	Quote next character

A number preceding a command repeats movement. Commands are also objects for change, delete and yank operations.

By Character or Line

h or ←	Left one character
j or ↓	Down one line
k or ↑	Up one line
l or →	Right one line

^	To first character of current line
0	To first position of current line
$	To end of current line
SPACE	Right one character
RETURN	First character of next line
+	First character of next line
-	First character of previous line
G	To last line in file
nG	To line number n
:n	To line number n
H	Home - top line on screen
M	Middle line on screen
L	Last line on screen
nH	To n lines after top line
nL	To n lines before last line

By Word

b	Back one word
B	Back one word (ignore punctuation)
e	End of next word
E	End of next word (ignore punctuation)
w	Start of next word
W	Start of next word (ignore punctuation)

By Sentence or Paragraph

(	Beginning of previous sentence
)	Beginning of next sentence
G	End of file
[[	Back one section
]]	Forward one section
{	Beginning of previous paragraph
}	Beginning of next paragraph

Scrolling the Screen

^B	Scroll back one screen
^F	Forward one screen
^D	Scroll forward half screen
^U	Scroll back half screen
^L	Clear and redraw screen
^R	Refresh screen
^E	Scroll up one line
^Y	Scroll down one line

Changing and Deleting Text

cw	Change word
cc	Change line
C	Change text from current position to end of line
3cl	Change three characters right of cursor
dd	Delete current line
ndd	Delete *n* lines
D	Delete remainder of line
dw	Delete a word
d}	Delete up to next paragraph
d^	Delete back to beginning of line
4dh	Delete four characters left of cursor
d/*pat*	Delete up to first occurrence of pattern
dn	Delete up to next occurrence of pattern
df*a*	Delete up to and including *a* on current line
dt*a*	Delete up to (not including) *a* on current line
dL	Delete up to last line on screen
dG	Delete to end of file
p	Insert last deleted text after cursor
P	Insert last deleted text before cursor
r*x*	Replace character with *x*
R*text*	Replace text beginning at cursor
s	Substitute character
S	Substitute entire line
u	Undo last change
U	Restore current line
x	Delete current cursor position
X	Delete back one character
.	Repeat last change
~	Reverse case

The vi Editor

Searching

/*text*	Search forward for *text*
n	Repeat previous search
N	Repeat search in opposite direction
/	Repeat forward search
?	Repeat previous search backward
?*text*	Search backward for *text*
/*text*/+*n*	Go to line *n* after /*text*
?*text*?-*n*	Go to line *n* before /*text*
%	Find match of current parenthesis, brace, or bracket
f*x*	Move ahead to *x* on current line
F*x*	Move back to *x* on current line
t*c*	Search forward before *c* in current line
T*c*	Search back after *c* in current line
,	Reverse search direction of last **f**, **F**, **t**, or **T**.
;	Repeat last character search (**f**, **F**, **t**, or **T**)

Copying and Moving

Y or yy	Copy current line to new buffer
"*x***yy**	Yank current line to buffer *x*
"*x***d**	Delete into buffer *x*
"*x***p**	Put contents of buffer *x*
yy	Copy current line
y]]	Copy up to next section heading
ye	Copy to end of word

Marking and Returning

m*x*	Mark current position with *x*
´*x*	Move cursor to *x*
`*x*	Move cursor to *x* of current line
´´	Return to previous mark or context after move

Editors

Interacting With UNIX

:r *file*	Read in contents of *file* after cursor
:r **!***cmd*	Read in output from command after cursor
:nr **!***cmd*	Read in output from command after line *n* (0 for top of file).
:!*cmd*	Run command then return
!*obj cmd*	Send object in buffer to UNIX command and replace with output
:n1,n2! *cmd*	Send lines *n1* through *n2* to command and replace with output
***n*!!cmd**	Send *n* lines to UNIX command and replace with output
!!	Repeat last system command
:sh	Create subshell; return to file with ^D
^?	Interrupt editor, resume with **fg** (not available in all versions).
^Z	Interrupt editor, resume with **fg** (not available in all versions).
:so *file*	Read and execute commands from *file*

Macros

:ab *in out*	Use *in* as abbreviation for *out*
:unab *in*	Remove abbreviation
:ab	List abbreviations
:map *c seq*	Map character *c* as sequence of commands
:unmap *c*	Disable map for character *c*
:map! *c seq*	Map character *c* to input mode sequence
:unmap! *c*	Disable input mode map
:map	List characters that are mapped

Miscellaneous Commands

^Q	Quote next character
<<	Shift lines left one shift width (default 8 spaces)
>>	Shift lines right one shift width (default 8 spaces)

The vi Editor

a	Append text after cursor.
A	Append text at end of line.
^A	Unused.
b	Back up to beginning of word in current line.
B	Back up to word, ignoring punctuation.
^B	Scroll backward one window.
c	Change operator.
C	Change to end of current line.
^C	Unused.
d	Delete operator.
D	Delete to end of current line.
^D	Scroll down half-window.
e	Move to end of word.
E	Move to end of word, ignoring punctuation.
^E	Show one more line at bottom of window.
f	Find next character typed forward on current line.
F	Find next character typed back on current line.
^F	Scroll Forward one window.
g	Unused.
G	Go to specified line or end of file.
^G	Print information about file on status line.
h	Left arrow cursor key.
H	Move cursor to Home position.
^H	Left arrow cursor key; backspace key in insert mode.
i	Insert text before cursor.
I	Insert text at beginning of line.
^I	Unused in command mode; in insert mode is same as TAB key.
j	Down arrow cursor key.
J	Join two lines.
^J	Down arrow cursor key.
k	Up arrow cursor key.
K	Unused.
^K	Unused.
l	Right arrow cursor key.
L	Move cursor to Last position in window.
^L	Redraw screen.
m	Mark the current cursor position in register (a-z).
M	Move cursor to Middle position in window.
^M	Carriage return.

Editors

n	Repeat the last search command.
N	Repeat the last search command in reverse direction.
^N	Down arrow cursor key.
o	Open line below current line.
O	Open line above current line.
^O	Unused.
p	Put yanked or deleted text after or below cursor.
P	Put yanked or deleted text before or above cursor.
^P	Up arrow cursor key.
q	Unused.
Q	Quit *vi* and invoke *ex*.
^Q	Unused in command mode; in input mode, quote next character.
r	Replace character at cursor with the next character you type.
R	Replace characters.
^R	Redraw the screen.
s	Change the character under the cursor to typed characters.
S	Change entire line.
^S	Unused.
t	Move cursor forward to character before next character typed.
T	Move cursor back to character after next character typed.
^T	Unused in command mode; in insert mode, used with *autoindent* option set.
u	Undo the last change made.
U	Restore current line, discarding changes.
^U	Scroll the screen upward half-window.
v	Unused.
V	Unused.
^V	Unused in command mode; in insert mode, quote next character.
w	Move to beginning of next word.
W	Move to beginning of next word, ignoring punctuation.
^W	Unused in command mode; in insert mode, back up to beginning of word.
x	Delete character under the cursor.
X	Delete character before cursor.
^X	Unused.
y	Yank or copy operator.
Y	Make copy of current line.
^Y	Show one more line at top of window.
z	Redraw the screen, repositioning cursor when followed by RETURN at the top, . at the middle, and - at the bottom of screen.
ZZ	Exit the editor, saving changes.
^Z	Unused.

Characters Not Used In Command Mode

The following characters are unused in command mode and can be mapped as user-defined commands.

^A	^C	g	^I
K	^K	^O	q
^Q	^S	^T	v
V	^V	^W	^X
^Z			

Editors

vi and ex Options

Options allow you to change characteristics of the editing environment.

Options may be put in the **.exrc** file or set during a *vi* session, using the **set** command:

:set *x*	Enable option
:set no*x*	Disable option
:set *x=val*	Give value *val*
:set	Show changed options
:set all	Show all options
:set *x*?	Show value of option *x*

(The colon should not be typed if the command is put in .exrc)

Available Options

The following options can be specified with the **set** command:

autoindent	Supply indent
autoprint	Display changes after each editor command
autowrite	Write before changing files
beautify	Ignores control characters during input
directory	Directory to store buffer file
edcompatible	Uses *ed* features
errorbells	Error messages ring bell
hardtabs	Sets terminal hardware tabs
ignorecase	Scan without regard to U/L case
lisp	Insert indents in lisp format
list	Print ^I for tab, $ at end
magic	. [* special in patterns
mesg	Permit messages to terminal
number	Display line numbers
open	Allow entry to *open* or *visual* mode
optimize	Abolish carriage returns when printing multiple lines
paragraphs	Macros for paragraphs
prompt	Set *ex* prompt
readonly	No write without !
redraw	Simulate smart terminal
remap	Retains nested map sequences
report	Specifies size for reporting changes
scroll	Amount of lines to scroll
sections	Provide macro names for sections
shell	Pathname for shell escape
shiftwidth	Set width of software tabstop
showmatch	When "(" or "{" is typed move cursor to next match of ")" or "}"
showmode	Print "input mode" when input mode is entered
tabstop	Set number of spaces indented by a tab

The vi Editor

taglength	Significant characters in tag
tags	Path of files for functions
term	Terminal type
terse	Brief error messages
timeout	Macros "time out" after one second
ttytype	Terminal type
warn	"No write since last change"
window	Show a certain number of lines on screen
wrapscan	Search past end of file
wrapmargin	Define right margin
writeany	Allows to save any file

Editors

The ex Editor

ex is a line editor that serves as the foundation for the screen editor, *vi*. *ex* commands work on the current line or a range of lines in a file. In *vi*, *ex* commands are preceded by a colon and entered by pressing RETURN. You can also invoke *ex* on its own just as you invoke *vi* or as you enter *ex* from *vi*.

The *vi* command "Q" can be used to quit the *vi* editor and enter *ex*.

To exit *ex*:

  :x   To exit, saving changes
  :q!   To quit, without saving changes

The *ex* command ":vi" can be used to quit *ex* and enter the *vi* editor.

To enter an *ex* command from *vi*:

  :[*address*] *command* [*options*]

An initial : indicates an ex command. The *address* is the line number or range of lines that are the object of the *command*.

Options:

  !   Indicates a variant form of the command.
  parameters
         Indicates that additional information can be supplied. A parameter can be the name of a file.
  count The number of times the command is to be repeated.
  flag "#", "p" and "l" indicate print format.

Unlike *vi* commands, the count cannot precede the command as it will be taken for the address. "d3" deletes three lines beginning with current line; "3d" deletes line 3. As you type the address and command, it is echoed on the status line. Enter the command by pressing the RETURN key.

Addresses

If no address is given, the current line is the object of the command. If the addresses specifies a range of lines, the format is:

  x,y

where x and y are the first and last addressed lines (x must precede y in buffer). x and y may be a line number or a primitive. Using ";" instead of "," sets the current line to x before interpreting y.

1,$ addresses all lines in the file.

Address Symbols

.	Current line
n	Absolute line number
$	Last line
%	All lines, same as "1,$"
x-|+n	n lines before or after x
-[n]	One or n lines previous
+[n]	One or n lines ahead
$'x$	Line marked with x
''	Previous context
/pat/ or ?pat?	Ahead or back to line matching *pat*

See Section 3 for more information on using patterns.

abbrev	**ab** [*string text*] Define *string* when typed to be translated into *text*. If *string* and *text* are not specified, list all current abbreviations.
append	[*address*] **a**[!] *text* . Append *text* at specified *address*, or at present address if none is specified. With the ! flag, toggle the **autoindent** setting during the input of *text*.
args	**ar** Print the members of the argument list, with the current argument printed within brackets ([ ]).
change	[*address*] **c**[!] *text* . Replace the specified lines with *text*. With the ! flag, toggle the **autoindent** setting during the input of *text*.
copy	[*address*] **co** *destination* Copy the lines included in *address* to the specified *destination* address. The command **t** is a synonym for **copy**.

[*address*] **d** [*buffer*]

Delete the lines included in *address*. If *buffer* is specified, save or append the text to the named buffer.

delete

---

e[!] [+*n*] *file*

Begin editing on *file*. If the ! flag is used, do not warn if the present file has not been saved since the last change. If the +*n* argument is used, begin editing on line *n*.

edit

---

f [*filename*]

Change the name of the current file to *filename*, which is considered "not edited". If no *filename* is specified, print the current status of the file.

file

[*address*] **g**[!]/*pattern*/[*commands*]

Execute *commands* on all lines which contain *pattern*, or if *address* is specified, all lines within that range. If *commands* are not specified, print all such lines. If the ! flag is used, execute *commands* on all lines *not* containing *pattern*.

global

[*address*] **i**[!]
text
.

Insert *text* at line before the specified address, or at present address if none is specified. With the ! flag, toggle the **autoindent** setting during the input of *text*.

insert

join	[*address*] **j** [*count*]
	Place the text in the specified range on one line, with white space adjusted to provide two blank characters after a ".", no blank characters if a ")" follows, and one blank character otherwise.
k	[*address*] **k** *char*
	Mark the given *address* with *char*. Return later to the line with **'x**.
list	[*address*] **l** [*count*]
	Print the specified lines in an unambiguous manner.
map	**map** *char commands*
	Define a macro named *char* in visual mode with the specified sequence of commands. *char* may be a single character, or the sequence *#n*, representing a function key on the keyboard.
mark	[*address*] **ma** *char*
	Mark the specified line with *char*, a single lower-case letter. Return later to the line with **'x**.
move	[*address*] **m** *destination*
	Move the lines specified by *address* to the *destination* address.

n[!] [[+*command*] *filelist*]   **next**

Edit the next file in the command line argument list. Use **args** for a listing of arguments. If *filelist* is provided, replace the current argument list with *filelist* and begin editing on the first file; if *command* is given (containing no spaces), execute *command* after editing the first such file.

[*address*] nu [*count*]   **number**

Print each line specified by *address* preceded by its buffer line number. # may be used as an abbreviation for **number** as well as **nu**.

[*address*] o [/*pattern*/]   **open**

Enter *open* mode at the lines specified by *address*, or lines matching *pattern*. Exit open mode with **Q**.

---

pre   **preserve**

Save the current editor buffer as though the system had crashed.

[*address*] p [*count*]   **print**

Print the lines specified by *address* with non-printing characters printed. **P** may also be used as an abbreviation.

[*address*] pu [*char*]   **put**

Restore previously deleted or yanked lines from named buffer specified by *char* to the line specified by *address*; if *char* is not specified, the last deleted or yanked text is restored.

---

quit	**q[!]** Terminate current editing session. If the file was not saved since the last change, or if there are files in the argument list that have not yet be accessed, you will not be able to quit without the **!** flag.
read	*[address]* **r[!]** *file* Copy the text of *file* at the specified *address*. If *file* is not specified, the current filename is used.
read	*[address]* **r !***command* Read in the output of *command* into the text after the line specified by *address*.
recover	**rec** *[file]* Recover *file* from system save area.
rewind	**rew[!]** Rewind argument list and begin editing the first file in the list. The **!** flag rewinds without warning if file has not been saved since the last change.
set	**se** *parameter parameter2* ... Set a value to an option with each *parameter*, or if no *parameter* is supplied, print all options that have been changed from their defaults. For Boolean-valued options, each *parameter* can be phrased as "*option*" or "**no***option*"; other options can be assigned with the syntax, "*option=value*"

sh	**shell**

Create a new shell. Resume editing when the shell is terminated.

---

so *file*	**source**

Read and execute commands from *file*.

[*address*] **s** [*/pattern/repl/*] [*options*] [*count*]	**substitute**

Replace each instance of *pattern* on the specified lines with *repl*. If *pattern* and *repl* are omitted, repeat last substitution.

options

  g   Substitute all instances of *pattern*.
  c   Prompt for confirmation before each change.

[*address*] **t** *destination*	**t**

Copy the lines included in *address* to the specified *destination* address.

[*address*] **ta** *tag*	**ta**

Switch the focus of editing to *tag*.

---

una *word*	**unabbreviate**

Remove *word* from the list of abbreviations.

---

undo	**u**
	Reverse the changes made by the last editing command.
unmap	**unm** *char*
	Remove *char* from the list of macros.
v	[*address*] **v**/*pattern*/[*commands*]
	Execute *commands* on all lines *not* containing *pattern*. If *commands* are not specified, print all such lines.
version	**ve**
	Print the current version number of the editor and the date the editor was last changed.
visual	[*address*] **vi** [*type*] [*count*]
	Enter visual mode at the line specified by *address*. Exit with **Q**.
	type
	-, ^, or . (See the **z** command).
	count
	Specify an initial window size.
visual	*vi* [+*n*] *file*
	Begin editing on *file* in visual mode.

[*address*] **w**[!] [[**>>**] *file*] Write lines specified by *address* to *file*, or full contents of buffer if *address* is not specified. If *file* is also omitted, save the contents of the buffer to the current filename. If >> *file* is used, write contents to the end of the specified *file*. The ! flag forces the editor to write over any current contents of *file*.	**write**
[*address*] **w** !*command* Write lines specified by *address* to *command*.	**write**
wq[!] Write and quit the file in one movement.	**wq**
x Write file if changes have been made to the buffer since last write, then quit.	**xit**
[*address*] **ya** [*char*] [*count*] Place lines specified by *address* in named buffer indicated by *char*, or if no *char* is specified place in general buffer.	**yank**
[*address*] **z** [*type*] [*count*] Print a window of text with line specified by *address* at the top. *type* + place specified line at the top of the window (default). ☞	**z**

Editors

z *continued*	- place specified line at bottom of the window. . place specified line in the center of the window. ^ print the window before the window associated with type -. = place specified line in the center of the window and leave the current line at this line. *count* Specifies the number of lines to be displayed.
!	[*address*] !*command* Execute *command* in a shell. If *address* is specified, apply the lines contained in *address* as standard input to *command*, and replace the lines with the output.
=	[*address*] = Print the line number of the line indicated by *address*.
< >	[*address*] < [*count*] or [*address*] > [*count*] Shift lines specified by *address* in specified direction. Only blanks and tabs are shifted in a left-shift (<).
address	*address* Print the lines specified in *address*.
RETURN	*RETURN* Print the next line in the file.

          The ex Editor

[*address*] **&** [*options*] [*count*]   **&**

Repeat the previous substitute command.

[*address*] **~** [*count*]   **~**

Replace the previous regular expression with the previous replacement pattern from a **substitute** command.

The sed Editor

sed [*options*] *file(s)*

The following options are recognized:

-n   only print lines specified with the **p** command, or the **p** flag of the **s**
      command
-e *cmd*   next argument is an editing command
-f *file*   next argument is a file containing editing commands

sed commands have the general form:

[*address*][,*address*][!]*command* [*arguments*]

sed copies each line of input into a pattern space. **sed** instructions consist of
addresses and editing commands. If the address of the command matches the
line in the pattern space, then the command is applied to that line. If a command has no address, then it is applied to each input line. It is important to note
that a command affects the contents of the space; subsequent command
addresses attempt to match the line in the pattern space, not the original input
line.

──Pattern Addressing──────────────────────

An *address* can either be a line number or a *pattern*, enclosed in slashes (/*pattern*/). Patterns can make use of regular expressions, as described in Section 3.
Additionally, "\n" can be used to match any newline in the pattern space (resulting from the N command), but not the newline at the end of the pattern
space. If no pattern is specified, *command* will be applied to all lines. If only
one address is specified, the command will be applied to all lines between the
first and second addresses, inclusively. Some commands can only accept one
address.

The ! operator following a pattern causes **sed** to apply the command to all lines
that do not contain the pattern.

A series of commands can be grouped after one pattern by enclosing the command list in curly braces:

[/*pattern*/][,/*pattern*/]{
command1
command2
}

:*label* Specify a label to be branched to by **b** or **t**. *label* may contain up to eight characters.	**:**
[/*pattern***/]=** Write to standard output the line number of each line addressed by *pattern*.	**=**
[*address***]a** *text* Append *text* following each line matched by *address*. If *text* goes over more than one line, newlines must be "hidden" by preceding them with a backslash. The insertion will be terminated by the first newline that is not hidden in this way. The results of this command are read into the pattern space (creating a multi-line pattern space) and sent to standard output when the list of editing commands is finished or a command explicitly prints the pattern space.	**a**
[*address1***][,***address2***]b[***label***]** Branch to *label* placed with **:** command, or if no *label*, to the end of the script. That is, *skip* all subsequent editing commands (up to *label*) for each addressed line.	**b**
[*address1***][,***address2***]c** *text* Replace pattern space with *text*. (See **a** for details on *text*.)	**c**

Editors

d	*[address1][,address2]***d** Delete line in pattern space. Thus, line is not passed to standard output and a new line of input is read; editing resumes with first command in list.
D	*[address1][address2]***D** Delete first part (up to embedded newline) of multi-line pattern created by **N** command and begin editing. Same as **d** if **N** has not been applied to a line.
g	*[address1][,address2]***g** Copy contents of hold space (see **h** or **H** command) into pattern space, wiping out previous contents.
G	*[address1][,address2]***G** Append contents of hold space (see **h** or **H** command) to contents of the pattern space.
h	*[address1][,address2]***h** Copy pattern space into hold space, a special buffer. Previous contents of hold space are obliterated.
H	*[address1][,address2]***H** Append pattern space to contents of the hold space. Previous and new contents are separated by a newline.

[*address1*]i\ *text* Insert *text* before each line matched by *address*. (See **a** for details on *text*.)	**i**
[*address1*],[*address2*]l List the contents of the pattern space, showing non-printing characters as ASCII codes. Long lines are wrapped.	**l**
[*address1*],[*address2*]n Read next line of input into pattern space. Current line is output but control passes to next editing command instead of beginning at top of list.	**n**
[*address1*],[*address2*]N Append next input line to contents of pattern space; the two lines are separated by an embedded newline. (This command is designed to allow pattern matches across two lines.)	**N**
[*address1*][,*address2*]p Print the addressed line(s). Unless the **-n** command line option is used, this command will cause duplication of the line in the output. Also, used when commands change flow control (*d*, N, b).	**p**
[*address1*][,*address2*]P Print first part (up to embedded newline) of multi-line pattern created by **N** command. Same as **p** if **N** has not been applied to a line.	**P**

q	**[*address*]q** Quit when *address* is encountered. The addressed line is first written to output, along with any text appended to it by previous **a** or **r** commands.
r	**[*address*]r** *file* Read contents of *file* and append after the contents of the pattern space. Exactly one space must separate the **r** and the filename.
s	**[*address1*][,*address2*]s/*pattern/replacement/*[*flags*]** Substitute *replacement* for *pattern* on each addressed line. If pattern addresses are used, the pattern // represents the last pattern address specified. The following flags can be specified: **g** replace all instances of /*pattern*/ on each addressed line, not just the first instance. **p** print the line if a successful substitution is done. If several successful substitutions are done, multiple copies of the line will be printed. **w** *file* write the line to a *file* if a replacement was done. A maximum of 10 different *files* can be opened.
t	**[*address1*][,*address2*]t** [*label*] Test if successful substitutions have been made on addressed lines, and if so, branch to *label*. (See **b** and :.) If label is not specified, drop to bottom of list of editing commands.
w	**[*address1*][,*address2*]w** *file* Write contents of pattern space to *file*. This action occurs when the command is encountered rather than

when the pattern space is output. Exactly one space must separate the **w** and the filename. A maximum of 10 different files can be opened.	**w** *continued*
[address1][*,address2*]**x** Exchange contents of the pattern space with the contents of the hold space.	**x**
[address1][*,address2*]**y**/*abc*/*xyz*/ Transform each character by position in string *abc* to its equivalent in string *xyz*.	**y**

Editors

awk

awk [*options*] [program] [parameters] [files]

awk is a pattern-matching "*program*" for modifying files. It takes the following options on the command line:
   -f *file*   use patterns contained in *file*.
   -F *c*   use field separator

awk also accepts parameters such as x=...y=... on the input line.

An *awk* program consists of patterns and procedures:

   pattern {*procedure*}

Both are optional. If *pattern* is missing, {*procedure*} will be applied to all lines. If {*procedure*} is missing, the line will be passed unaffected to standard output (i.e., it will be printed as is).

Each input line, or *record*, is divided into *fields* by white space (blanks or tabs) or by some other user-definable record separator. Fields are referred to by the variables **$1, $2, . . . , $n. $0** refers to the entire record.

Shell variables can be passed as parameters inside an *awk* program.

   FILE = $File

passes the value of the shell variable *File* into an *awk* variable named *FILE*.

Patterns

Patterns can be specified using regular expressions as described in Section 3.

   pattern {*procedure*}

- The special pattern **BEGIN** allows you to specify procedures that will take place *before* the first input line is processed. (Generally, you set global variables here.)

- The special pattern **END** allows you to specify procedures that will take place *after* the last input record is read.

- ^ and $ can be used to refer to the beginning and end of a field, respectively, rather than the beginning and end of a line.

- A pattern can evaluate expressions using any of the relational operators <, <=, ==, !=, >=, and > or pattern matching operators ~ and ~!. For example: **$2 > $1** selects lines for which the second field is greater than the first. Comparisons can be either string or numeric.

- Patterns can be combined with the Boolean operators || (or), && (and), and ! (not).

- Patterns can include any of the predefined special variables listed below. For example: **NF > 1** selects records with more than one field.

Special Variables

FS	field separator (blanks and tabs by default)
RS	record separator (newline by default)
OFS	output field separator (blanks by default)
ORS	output record separator (newline by default)
NR	number of current record
NF	number of fields in current record
$0	entire input record
$1, $2, ..., $n	first, second, ... nth field in current record, where fields are separated by **FS**.

Procedures

Procedures consist of one or more commands, functions, or variable assignments, separated by newlines or semicolons, and contained within curly braces. Commands fall into four groups:

- variable or array assignments

- printing commands

- built-in functions

- control-flow commands

Variables and Array Assignments

Variables can be assigned a value with an = sign. For example:

    FS = ","

Expressions using the operators +, -, /, and % (modulo) can be assigned to variables.

Arrays can be created with the **split** function (see below) or can be simply named in an assignment statement. **++**, **+=**, and **-=** are used to increment or decrement an array, as in the C language. Array elements can be subscripted with numbers (*array*[1], ... ,*array*[n]) or with names. For exam-

Editors

ple, to count the number of occurrences of a pattern, you could use the following program:

```
/pattern/ {n["/pattern/"]++}
END {print n["/pattern/"] }
```

String constants such as *filenames* must be quoted. Shell variables can be referred to by placing the variables inside double quotes, then single quotes: **"'$LOGNAME'"**.

break	**break**
Exit from a while or for loop.	

continue	**continue**
Begin next iteration of while or for loop without reaching the bottom.	

exit	**exit**
Do not execute remaining instruction and read no new input. END procedures will be executed.	

$x = \mathbf{exp}(arg)$	**exp**
Return exponent of *arg*.	

for *(i=lower;i<=upper;i++)* *command*	**for**
While the value of variable *i* is in the range between *lower* and *upper*, do *command*. A series of commands must be put within braces. "<=" or any relational operator can be used; "++" or "--" can be used to decrement variable.	

for *(item* in *array)* *command*	**for**
For each *item* in an associative *array*, do *command*. More than one command must be put inside braces. Refer to each element of the array as *array*[*item*].	

Editors

if	**if** *(condition)*
	    command
	[**else**]
	    [*command*]
	
	If *condition* is true, do *command(s)*, otherwise do *command* in **else** clause. Condition can be an expression using any of the relational operators <, <=, ==, !=, >=, or >, as well as the pattern-matching operator ~ (e.g. "**if** **$1** ~ /[Aa].*/"). A series of commands must be put within braces.

int	*x* = **int**(*arg*) Return integer value of *arg*.
length	*x* = **length**(*arg*) Return the length of *arg*. If *arg* is not supplied, **$0** is assumed. Therefore, **length** can be used as a predefined variable that contains the length of the current record.
log	*x* = **log**(*arg*) Return logarithm of *arg*.
next	**next** Read next input line and start new cycle through pattern/procedures statements.
print	**print** [*args*] Print *args* on output. *Args* is usually one or more fields, but may also be one or more of the predefined variables. Literal strings must be quoted. Fields are

printed in the order they are listed. If separated by commas in the argument list, they are separated in the output by the character specified by **OFS**. If separated by spaces, they are concatenated in the output.

printf

Formatted print statement. Fields or variables can be formatted according to instructions in the *format* argument. The number of arguments must correspond to the number specified in the format sections.

Format follows the conventions of the C-language *printf* statement. Here are a few of the most common formats:

%s   a string

%d   a decimal number

%*n.m*d   a floating point number; n = total number of digits. m = number of digits after decimal point.

%[-]*n*c n specifies minimum field length for format type c, while - justifies value in field; otherwise value is right justified.

Format can also contain embedded escape sequences: **\n** (newline) or **\t** (tab) being the most common.

Spaces and literal text can be placed in the *format* argument by quoting the entire argument. If there are multiple expressions to be printed, there should be multiple formats specified. An example is worth a thousand words. For an input file containing only the line:

    5 5

The program:

    {printf ("The sum on line %s is %d \n", NR, $1+$2)}

will produce:

    The sum on line 1 is 10.

followed by a newline.

split	$x = $ **split**(*string*,*array*[,*sep*])
	Split string into elements of array **array[1],...,array[n]**. String is split at each occurrence of separator *sep*. If *sep* is not specified, FS is used. The number of array elements created is returned.
sprintf	$x = $ **sprintf**("*format*", *expression*)
	Return the value of *expression*(s), using the specified *format* (see **printf**).
sqrt	$x = $ **sqrt**(*arg*)
	Return square root of *arg*.
substr	$x = $ **substr**(*string*,*m*,[*n*])
	Return substring of *string* beginning at character position *m* and consisting of the next *n* characters. If *n* is omitted, include all characters to the end of string.
while	**while** *(condition)* command
	Do *command* while *condition* is true (see **if** for a description of allowable conditions). A series of commands must be put within braces.

5

Nroff and Troff

This section is divided into four subsections, each covering a different facet of the *nroff/troff* formatting system. These sections are:

- *nroff/troff* requests.
- Escape sequences.
- Predefined number registers.
- Special characters.

See Section 1 for command line options for the various commands.

nroff and *troff* are UNIX's postprocessing programs for formatting text files. *nroff* is designed to format output for line and letter-quality printers, *troff* for typesetting. Except for some functions that are specific to typesetting, the same commands work for both programs.

In addition, we make references to *ditroff*, or *device-independent troff*, which is a later version of *troff*. For the most part, *ditroff* works the same as *troff*; where there are distinctions, the original *troff* is referred to as *otroff*.

Formatting is specified by embedding brief codes into the text source file. These codes act as directives to *nroff* and *troff* when they are invoked. A typical code, to center the following line of text, would be typed in as follows:

```
.ce
This text should be centered.
```

The output would appear as follows:

This text should be centered.

There are two types of formatting codes, referred to respectively as *primitives* and *macros*. The primitives (also called *requests*) allow direct control of almost any feature of page layout and formatting; however, they are sometimes difficult to use. The macros are predefined combinations of primitives designed to create a total effect.

See Section 6 for more information on macros.

.ab [*text*]

.ab

Abort and print *text* as message. If *text* is not specified, the message "User Abort" is printed.

.ad [*c*]

.ad

Adjust one or both margins. *c* can be:
  b or **n** adjust both margins.
  c   center all lines.
  l   adjust left margin only.
  r   adjust right margin only.

Without argument, return to previous adjustment. The current adjustment mode is stored in register .j, with the following values: 0=l, 1=b, 3=c, 5=r. (See **.na**).

.af *r c*

.af

Assign format *c* to register *r*. *c* can be:
  1   0, 1, 2, etc.
  001   000, 001, 002, etc.
  i   lowercase Roman.
  I   uppercase Roman.
  a   lowercase alphabetic.
  A   uppercase alphabetic.

.am *xx* [*yy*]

.am

Append to macro *xx*; end append at call of *yy* {Default *yy*=..}.

Nroff/Troff

.as	**.as** *xx string* Append *string* to string register *xx*. *string* may contain spaces, and is terminated by a newline. An initial quote (") is ignored.
.bd	**.bd** [s] *f n* Overstrike characters in font *f n* times, or if **s** is specified, characters in special font *n* times when font *f* is in effect.
.bp	**.bp** [*n*] Begin new page. Number next page *n*.
.br	**.br** Break to a new line (output partial line).
.c2	**.c2** *c* Set no-break control character to *c*. (Certain requests beginning with . cause a break; starting these requests with *c* will not cause a break.) {Default is '}.
.cc	**.cc** *c* Set control character that introduces requests and macros to *c*. {Default is .}.

.ce [*n*]

Center next *n* lines; if *n* is 0, stop centering. *n* applies only to lines containing output text. Blank lines do not count. {Default *n*=1}.

.cf *file*

Copy contents of file into output, uninterpreted (*ditroff* only).

.ch *xx* [*n*]

Change trap position for macro *xx* to *n*. If *n* is absent, remove the trap.

.cs *f n m*

Use constant spacing for font *f*. Constant character width will be *n*/36 ems. If *m* is given, the em is taken to be *m* points.

.cu [*n*]

Continuous underline (including inter-word spaces) on next *n* lines. If *n* is 0, stop underlining (italicize in *troff*). Use **.ul** to underline visible characters only. Underline font can be switched in *troff* with **.uf** request. However, you must use a macro to underline in *troff*.

.da [*xx*]

Divert following text, appending it to macro *xx*. If no argument, end diversion.

Nroff/Troff

.de	**.de** *xx* [*yy*] Define macro *xx*. End definition at *yy*. {Default *yy*=..}
.di	**.di** [*xx*] Divert following text to newly defined macro *xx*. If no argument, end diversion.
.ds	**.ds** *xx string* Define *xx* to contain *string*.
.dt	**.dt** *n xx* Install diversion trap at position *n* within diversion to invoke macro *xx*.
.ec	**.ec** [*c*] Set escape character to *c*. {Default \}
.el	**.el** Else portion of **if-else** (See **.ie** below).
.em	**.em** *xx* Set end macro to be *xx*. *xx* will automatically be executed when all other output has been completed.

.eo

Turn escape character mechanism off. All escape characters will be printed literally.

.ev [*n*]

Change environment to *n*. If no argument, restore previous environment. 0≤*n*≤2 {initial value 0}. You must return to the previous environment by using .ev with no argument, or you will get a stack overflow.

.ex

Exit from formatter and perform no further text processing. Typically used with **.nx** for form-letter generation.

.fc *a b*

Set field delimiter to *a* and pad character to *b*.

.fi

Turn on fill mode. {Default is on} (See **.nf**).

.fl

Flush output buffer. Used for interactive debugging.

.fp *n f*

Assign font *f* to position *n*. In *otroff*, *n* is from 1 to 4. In *ditroff*, it is from 1 to 9.

.ft	**.ft** *f* Change font to *f*, where *f* is a one- or two-character font name, or a font position assigned with **.fp**.
.hc	**.hc** [*c*] Change hyphenation-indication character to *c*. {Default –}
.hw	**.hw** *words* Specify hyphenation points for *words*. (e.g. **.hw spe-ci-fy**).
.hy	**.hy** *n* Turn hyphenation on ($n\geq1$) or off ($n=0$).

.hy

.hy *n*

Turn hyphenation on ($n\geq1$) or off ($n=0$).

$n=1$	hyphenate whenever necessary
$n=2$	don't hyphenate last word on page
$n=4$	don't split off first two characters
$n=8$	don't split off last two characters
$n=14$	use all three restrictions

(See **.nh**).

.ie

.ie [!]*condition anything*
.el *anything*

If portion of *if-else*. If *condition* is true, do *anything*. Otherwise do *anything* following **.el** request. **.ie/.el** pairs can be nested. Syntax for *condition* is as described below under **.if**.

.if

.if [!]*condition anything*

If *condition* is true, do *anything*. The presence of an ! negates the condition. The following conditions can be used:

.if
continued

o	true if the page number is odd
e	true if the page number is even
n	true if the processor is **nroff**
t	true if the processor is **troff**
"*str1*"*str2*"	true if *str1* is identical to *str2*. (Often used to test the value of arguments passed to a macro.)
expr	true if the value of expression *expr* is greater than zero

Expressions typically contain number register interpolations, and can use any of the following operators:

+,-,/,*	standard arithmetic operators
%	modulo
>,<	greater than, less than
>=,<=	greater than or equal, less than or equal
=,==	equal
&	logical AND
:	logical OR

If *anything* runs over more than one line, it can be delimited by \{ and \}.

.ig [*yy*]

.ig

Ignore following text, up to line beginning with *yy*. Default *yy* is .., as with **.de**. Useful for commenting out large blocks of text or macro definition.

.in [±][*n*]

.in

Set indent to *n* or increment indent by ±*n*. If no argument, restore previous indent. Current indent is stored in register .i.

.it *n xx*

.it

Set input line count trap to invoke macro *xx* after *n* lines of input text have been read.

Nroff/Troff

.lc	.lc *c*
	Set leader repetition character to *c*.
.lg	.lg *n*
	Turn ligature mode on if *n* is absent or non-zero.
.ll	.ll [±][*n*]
	Set line length to *n* or increment line length by ±*n*. If no argument, restore previous line length. Current line length is stored in register .l.{Default 6.5 inches}
.ls	.ls [*n*]
	Set line spacing to *n*. If no argument, restore previous line spacing. {Initial value 1}
.lt	.lt [*n*]
	Set title length to *n*. If no argument, restore previous value.
.mc	.mc [*c*] [*n*]
	Set margin character to *c*, and place it *n* spaces to the right of margin. If *c* is missing, turn margin character off. If *n* is missing, use previous value. Initial value for *n* is .2 inches in *nroff* and 1 em in *troff*.
.mk	.mk [*r*]
	Mark current vertical place in register *r*. Return to mark with .rt or .sp|\ n*r*.

.na   **.na**

Do not adjust margins (See **.ad**). Current adjustment
mode is stored in register **.j**.

.ne *n*   **.ne**

If *n* lines do not remain on this page, start new page.

.nf   **.nf**

Do not fill or adjust output lines (See **.ad** and **.fi**).

.nh   **.nh**

Turn hyphenation off (See **.hy**).

Nroff/Troff

.nm [*n m s i*]   **.nm**

Number output lines (*n*≥0) or turn it off (*n*=0). ±*n*
sets initial line number; *m* sets numbering interval; *s*
sets separation of numbers and text; *i* sets indent of
text. (See **.nn**).

.nn *n*   **.nn**

Do not number next *n* lines, but keep track of
numbering sequence, which can be resumed with
.nm+0. (See **.nm**).

.nr *r n* [*m*]   **.nr**

Assign the value *n* to number register *r* and optionally set auto increment to *m*.

.ns	.ns Turn no-space mode on (See .rs).
.nx	.nx *file* Switch to *file* and do not return to current file (See .so).
.os	.os Output saved space specified in previous .sv request.
.pc	.pc *c* Set page number character to *c*.
.pi	.pi *cmd* Pipe output to *cmd* instead of placing it on standard output (*ditroff* and *nroff* only).
.pl	.pl [±][*n*] Set page length to *n* or increment page length by ±*n*. If no argument, restore default. Current page length is stored in register .p. {Default 11 inches}
.pm	.pm Print names and sizes of all defined macros.

.pn [±][*n*]   **.pn**

Set next page number to *n* or increment page number
by ±*n*. Current page number is stored in register %.

.po [±][*n*]   **.po**

Offset text a distance of *n* from left edge of page, or
else increment the current offset by ±*n*. If no argument, return to previous offset. Current page offset is
stored in register **.o**.

.ps *n*   **.ps**

Set point size to *n* (*troff* only). Current point size is
stored in register **.s**. {Default 10 points}

.rd [*prompt*]   **.rd**

Read input from terminal, after printing optional
prompt.

.rm *xx*   **.rm**

Remove macro or string *xx*.

.rn *xx yy*   **.rn**

Rename request, macro, or string *xx* to *yy*.

.rr *r*   **.rr**

Remove register *r*.

Nroff/Troff

.rs	.rs Restore spacing (turn no-space mode off — see **.ns**).
.rt	.rt [±*n*] Return (upward only) to marked vertical place, or to ±*n* from top of page or diversion (See **.mk**).
.so	.so *file* Switch out to *file*, then return to current file (See **.nx**).
.sp	.sp *n* Leave *n* blank lines. {Default is 1}
.ss	.ss *n* Set space-character size to *n*/36 em (no effect in *nroff*).
.sv	.sv *n* Save *n* lines of space; output saved space with **.os**.
.sy	.sy *cmd* [*args*] Execute UNIX command *cmd* with optional arguments (*ditroff* only).

.ta *n*[*t*] *m*[*t*] ...

Set tabstops at positions *n*, *m*, etc. If *t* is not given, tab is left-adjusting; *t* can be:
  L   left adjust.
  R   right adjust.
  C   center.

.tc *c*

Define tab output character as *c* (e.g., **.tc** . will draw a string of dots to tab position). {Default is white space}

.ti [±][*n*]

Indent next output line *n* spaces, or increment the current indent by ±*n* for the next output line.

Nroff/Troff

.tl '*l*'*c*'*r*'

Specify left, centered, or right title. Title length is specified by **.lt**, not **.ll**.

.tm *text*

Terminal message. (Print *text* on standard error.)

.tr *ab*

Translate character *a* to *b*.

.uf	.uf *f* Set underline font to *f* (to be switched to by **.ul** or **.cu**). {Default is *italics*}
.ul	.ul [*n*] Underline (italicize in *troff*) next *n* input lines. Do not underline inter-word spaces. Use **.cu** for continuous underline. Underline font can be switched in *troff* with **.uf** request. However, you must use a macro to underline in *troff*.
.vs	.vs [*n*] Set vertical line spacing to *n*. If no argument, restore previous spacing. Current vertical spacing is stored in register **.v**. {Default 1/6 inch in *nroff*, 12 points in *troff*}
.wh	.wh *n* [*xx*] When position *n* is reached, execute macro *xx*; negative values are with respect to page bottom. If *xx* is not supplied, remove any trap(s) at that location. (Two traps can be at the same location if one is moved over the other with **.ch**. They cannot be placed at the same location with **.wh**.)

Sequence	Effect
\\	To prevent or delay the interpretation of \
\e	Printable version of the current \ escape character
\'	´ (acute accent); equivalent to \(aa
\`	` (grave accent); equivalent to \(ga
\-	– Minus sign in the current font
\.	Period (dot)
\(space)	Unpaddable space-size space character
\(newline)	Concealed (ignored) newline
\0	Digit width space
|	1/6-em narrow space character (zero width in *nroff*)
\^	1/12-em half-narrow space character (zero width in *nroff*)
\&	Non-printing, zero width character
\!	Transparent line indicator
\"	Beginning of comment
\$n	Interpolate argument $1 \leq n \leq 9$
\%	Default optional hyphenation character
\(xx	Character named xx
*x, *(xx	Interpolate string x or xx
\a	Non-interpreted leader character
\b´abc...´	Bracket building function
\c	Make next line continuous with current
\d	Forward (down) 1/2-em vertical motion (1/2 line in *nroff*)
\D´l x,y´	Draw a line from current position to coordinates x,y. (*ditroff* only)
\D´c d´	Draw circle of diameter d with left edge at current position. (*ditroff* only)
\D´e dl d2´	Draw ellipse with horizontal diameter d1 and vertical diameter d2, with left edge at current position. (*ditroff* only)
\D´a x1 y1 x2 y2´	Draw arc counterclockwise from current position, with center at x1,y1 and endpoint at x1+x2,y1+y2. (*ditroff* only)
\D´~ x1 y1 x2 y2 ...´	Draw spline from current position through the specified coordinates. (*ditroff* only)
\fx,\f(xx,\fn	Change to font named x or xx or to position n
\h´n´	Local horizontal motion; move right n or if n is negative move left

Sequence	Effect
\H'n'	Set character height to n points, without changing width. (ditroff only)
\kx	Mark horizontal input place in register x
\l'nc'	Draw horizontal line of length n (optionally with c)
\L'nc'	Draw vertical line of length n (optionally with c)
\nx,\n(xx	Interpolate number register x or xx
\o'abc...'	Overstrike characters a, b, c...
\p	Break and spread output line
\r	Reverse 1-em vertical motion (reverse line in nroff)
\sn,\s±n	Change point-size to n or increment by n. \s0 returns to previous point size.
\S'n'	Slant output n degrees to the right. Negative values slant to the left. A value of zero turns off slanting. (ditroff only)
\t	Non-interpreted horizontal tab
\u	Reverse (up) 1/2-em vertical motion (1/2 line in nroff)
\v'n'	Local vertical motion; move down n or if n is negative move up
\w'string'	Interpolate width of string
\x'n'	Extra line-space function (n negative provides space before, n positive provides after)
\zc	Print c with zero width (without spacing)
\{	Begin multi-line conditional input
\}	End multi-line conditional input
\x	x, any character not listed above

Predefined Number Registers

Read-Only Registers

.$	Number of arguments available at the current macro level
.$$	Process id of *troff* process (*ditroff* only)
.A	Set to 1 in *troff*, if -a option used; always 1 in *nroff*
.H	Available horizontal resolution in basic units
.T	Set to 1 in *nroff*, if -T option used; always 0 in *troff*; in *ditroff*, the string *(.T contains the value of -T.
.V	Available vertical resolution in basic units
.a	Post-line extra line-space most recently utilized using \x'N'
.c	Number of *lines* read from current input file
.d	Current vertical place in current diversion; equal to nl, if no diversion
.f	Current font as physical quadrant (1 to 4 in *otroff*; 1 to 9 in *ditroff*)
.h	Text base-line high-water mark on current page or diversion
.i	Current indent
.j	Current adjustment mode
.l	Current line length
.n	Length of text portion on previous output line
.o	Current page offset
.p	Current page length
.s	Current point size
.t	Distance to the next trap
.u	Equal to 1 in fill mode and 0 in no-fill mode
.v	Current vertical line spacing
.w	Width of previous character
.x	Reserved version-dependent register
.y	Reserved version-dependent register
.z	Name of current diversion

Nroff/Troff

%	Current page number
ct	Character type (set by *width* function)
dl	Width (maximum) of last completed diversion
dn	Height (vertical size) of last completed diversion
dw	Current day of the week (1 to 7)
dy	Current day of the month (1 to 31)
hp	Current horizontal place on *input* line
ln	Output line number
mo	Current month (1 to 12)
nl	Vertical position of last printed text base line
sb	Depth of string below base line (generated by *width* function)
st	Height of string above base line (generated by *width* function)
yr	Last two digits of current year

On the Standard Fonts

Char	Input	Character Name
,	´	close quote
‘	`	open quote
—	\(em	3/4 Em dash
-	–	hyphen or
-	\(hy	hyphen
–	\-	current font minus
•	\(bu	bullet
□	\(sq	square
_	\(ru	rule
¹/₄	\(14	1/4
¹/₂	\(12	1/2
³/₄	\(34	3/4
fi	\(fi	fi ligature
fl	\(fl	fl ligature
ff	\(ff	ff ligature
ffi	\(Fi	ffi ligature
ffl	\(Fl	ffl ligature
°	\(de	degree
†	\(dg	dagger
′	\(fm	foot mark
¢	\(ct	cent sign
®	\(rg	registered
©	\(co	copyright

The Special Font

Miscellaneous Characters

Char	Input	Character Name
§	\(sc	section
´	\(aa	acute accent
`	\(ga	grave accent
_	\(ul	underrule
→	\(->	right arrow
←	\(<-	left arrow
↑	\(ua	up arrow
↓	\(da	down arrow
|	\(br	box rule
‡	\(dd	double dagger
☞	\(rh	right hand
☜	\(lh	left hand
○	\(ci	circle
⊕	\(vs	visible space indicator (*ditroff* only)

Bracket Building Symbols

Char	Input	Character Name
⎧	\(lt	left top of big curly bracket
⎨	\(lk	left center of big curly bracket
⎩	\(lb	left bottom of big curly bracket
⎫	\(rt	right top of big curly bracket
⎬	\(rk	right center of big curly bracket
⎭	\(rb	right bottom of big curly bracket
⎡	\(lc	left ceiling (left top) of big square bracket
|	\(bv	bold vertical
⎣	\(lf	left floor left bottom of big square bracket
⎤	\(rc	right ceiling (right top) of big square bracket
⎦	\(rf	right floor (right bottom) of big square bracket

Char	Input	Character Name
+	\(pl	math plus
−	\(mi	math minus
=	\(eq	math equals
*	\(**	math star
/	\(sl	slash (matching backslash)
√	\(sr	square root
	\(rn	root en extender
≥	\(>=	greater than or equal to
≤	\(<=	less than or equal to
≡	\(==	identically equal
≈	\(~~	approx equal
~	\(ap	approximates
≠	\(!=	not equal
×	\(mu	multiply
÷	\(di	divide
±	\(+-	plus-minus
∪	\(cu	cup (union)
∩	\(ca	cap (intersection)
⊂	\(sb	subset of
⊃	\(sp	superset of
⊆	\(ib	improper subset
⊇	\(ip	improper superset
∞	\(if	infinity
∂	\(pd	partial derivative
∇	\(gr	gradient
¬	\(no	not
∫	\(is	integral sign
∝	\(pt	proportional to
∅	\(es	empty set
∈	\(mo	member of
|	\(or	or

Char	Input	Char Name	Char	Input	Char Name
α	\(*a	alpha	A	\(*A	ALPHA
β	\(*b	beta	B	\(*B	BETA
γ	\(*g	gamma	Γ	\(*G	GAMMA
δ	\(*d	delta	Δ	\(*D	DELTA
ε	\(*e	epsilon	E	\(*E	EPSILON
ζ	\(*z	zeta	Z	\(*Z	ZETA
η	\(*y	eta	H	\(*Y	ETA
θ	\(*h	theta	Θ	\(*H	THETA
ι	\(*i	iota	I	\(*I	IOTA
κ	\(*k	kappa	K	\(*K	KAPPA
λ	\(*l	lambda	Λ	\(*L	LAMBDA
μ	\(*m	mu	M	\(*M	MU
ν	\(*n	nu	N	\(*N	NU
ξ	\(*c	xi	Ξ	\(*C	XI
o	\(*o	omicron	O	\(*O	OMICRON
π	\(*p	pi	Π	\(*P	PI
ρ	\(*r	rho	P	\(*R	RHO
σ	\(*s	sigma	Σ	\(*S	SIGMA
ς	\(ts	terminal sigma			
τ	\(*t	tau	T	\(*T	TAU
υ	\(*u	upsilon	Y	\(*U	UPSILON
φ	\(*f	phi	Φ	\(*F	PHI
χ	\(*x	chi	X	\(*X	CHI
ψ	\(*q	psi	Ψ	\(*Q	PSI
ω	\(*w	omega	Ω	\(*W	OMEGA

6

Macro Packages

This section is divided into two subsections, covering a different macro package of the *nroff/troff* formatting system. These sections are:

- The *-ms* macro package.
- The *-me* macro package.

Macros are predefined combinations of primitives designed to create a total effect. For example, a macro might specify the format for a heading by defining (in *troff*) the font size and style, the amount of space above and below, and some form of automatic section numbering.

Macro packages are organized, internally consistent groups of macros. There are three widely-available macro packages: *-mm*, *-ms*, and *-me*. They are named by the *nroff/troff* options that invoke them.

-mm is officially a part of System V, therefore it is not documented in this edition. The version of *-ms* that is documented here is the extended version of *-ms* shipped with Berkeley UNIX systems, not the the original Bell Labs *-ms* macros, which are no longer officially supported by AT&T.

See Section 5 for more information on *nroff/troff* primitives, escape sequences, special characters, and number registers.

-ms Macros

This section documents the extended version of *-ms* shipped with Berkeley UNIX systems, not the the original Bell Labs *-ms* macros, which are no longer officially supported by AT&T.

.1C	**.1C** Return to single-column format. This macro necessarily causes a page break as well. (See **.2C** and **.MC**).
.2C	**.2C** Start two-column format. Return to single-column with **.1C**.
.AB	**.AB** Begin abstract in cover sheet. End abstract with **.AE**.
.AE	**.AE** End abstract begun with **.AB**.
.AI	**.AI** *name* Print name of author's institution. Generally follows **.AU** in a cover sheet sequence; may be repeated up to nine times for multiple author/institution pairs.
.AU	**.AU** *name* Print author's name. Generally follows **.TL** and precedes **.AI** in a cover sheet sequence; may be repeated

up to nine times for multiple authors.	**.AU** *continued*
.B [*text*] Print *text* in boldface. If *text* is missing, equivalent to **.ft 3**.	**.B**
.B1 Enclose following text in a box. End box with **.B2**.	**.B1**
.B2 End boxed text. (See **.B1**).	**.B2**
.BD Start block display. Display text is printed exactly as it appears in the source file, centered around the longest line. (Same as **.DS B**.) End with **.DE**.	**.BD**
.BR Start bibliographic format (used to precede bibliographic record).	**.BR**
.BX *word* Surround *word* in a box. It generally does not work for more than one word at a time, due to problems with filling. To box more than one word, separate them with an unpaddable space (\ ).	**.BX**

Macros

.CD	**.CD**
	Start centered display. Each line in the display is individually centered. (Same as **.DS C**.) End with **.DE**.
.DA	**.DA**
	Print today's date as the center footer of each page.
.DE	**.DE**
	End displayed text.
.DS	**.DS** [*type*]
	Start displayed text. End with **.DE**.
	type
	B left-justified block, centered (See **.BD**).
	C centered display (See **.CD**).
	I indented display (See **.ID**). {Default}
	L left-centered display (See **.LD**).
.EQ	**.EQ**
	Begin equation to be processed by *eqn*. End with **.EN**. See Section 7 for more information on *eqn*.
.EN	**.EN**
	End equation. (See **.EQ**).

.FS	**.FS**
Start footnote. Text of footnote follows on succeeding lines. End with .FE.	
.FE	**.FE**
End footnote. (See .FS).	
.GO	**.GO**
Start processing text. This macro performs various package startup procedures. Cover sheet macros should precede .GO to appear on a separate page.	
.I [*text*]	**.I**
Print *text* in italics. If *text* is missing, equivalent to .ft 2.	
.ID	**.ID**
Start indented display. Text is printed exactly as it is in the source file, but indented 8 ens. (Same as .DS I). End with .DE.	
.IP *label n*	**.IP**
Indent paragraph *n* spaces with hanging *label*. .RS and .RE can be used for nested indents.	
.KE	**.KE**
End of keep or floating keep. (See .KF and .KS).	

Macros

.KF	**.KF** Begin floating keep. End with **.KE**. Enclosed text will stay on the same page, and if it will not fit on the current page, succeeding text will "float" above it in the output.
.KS	**.KS** Start keep. End with **.KE**. Enclosed text will stay on the same page. If text will not fit on the current page, a page break will occur.
.LD	**.LD** Start left-justified display. Block is centered, but individual lines are left justified in the block. (Same as **.DS L**.) End with **.DE**.
.LG	**.LG** Increase type size by two points (*troff* only). Restore normal type with **.NL**.
.LP	**.LP** Start block paragraph. Interparagraph spacing determined by register **PD** {Default .5v in *troff*, 1 line in *nroff*}
.MC	**.MC** *cw gw* Start multi-column mode, with column-width *cw* and gutter width *gw*. As many columns will be generated as will fit in the current line length. Return to single-column mode with **.1C**.

.ND

Suppress printing of date. (See **.DA**)

.ND

.NH *n*
heading text

Numbered section heading; level *n* of the section number is automatically incremented.

.NH

.NL

Restore default type size (*troff* only). Used after **.LG** or **.SM**.

.NL

.PP

Start standard indented paragraph. Size of paragraph indent is stored in register **PI** {Default 5 ens}.

.PP

Macros

.QE

End quoted paragraph. See **.QP** and **.QS**.

.QE

.QP

Quoted paragraph: indented on both sides, with blank lines above and below, and (in *troff*) with the type size reduced by 1 point.

.QP

.QS

Quoted paragraph, retaining current point size and vertical spacing. End with **.QE**.

.QS

.R	**.R** [*text*] Print *text* in Roman. If *text* is missing, equivalent to **.ft R**.
.RE	**.RE** End one level of relative indent. (See **.RS**).
.RP	**.RP** Initiate title page for a "released paper."
.RS	**.RS** Right Shift. Increase relative indent one level. End with **.RE**. Often used with **.IP**.
.SB	**.SB** *word chars* Subscript *word* with *chars*. (See **.SU**).
.SG	**.SG** Print a signature line.
.SH	**.SH** *heading text* Unnumbered section heading.

.SM

Change to smaller type size (*troff* only). Restore normal type with .NL.

.SU *word chars*

Superscript *word* with *chars*. (See .SB).

.TE

End table to be processed by *tbl*. (See .TS).

.TH

End of table header. Must be used with .TS H.

.TL
multiple line title

Title line(s) for cover sheet. A multi-line title can be specified; it is terminated by the next macro (usually .AU in the cover sheet sequence.

.TS [H]

Start table to be processed by *tbl*. End table with .TE. See Section 7 for more information on *tbl*.
    H   put table header on all pages. End entry of table header with .TH.

.UL

Underline following text, even in *troff*.

BI	Bibliographical indent. {Default 3 ens}
CW	Column width. {Default 7/15 of line length}
FL	Footnote length. {Default 11/12 of line length}
FM	Bottom margin. {Default 1 inch}
GW	Intercolumn gap. {Default 1/15 of line length}
HM	Top margin. {Default 1 inch}
LL	Line length. {Default 6 inches}
LT	Title length. {Default 6 inches}
PD	Paragraph spacing. {Default 0.3 of vertical spacing}
PI	Paragraph indent. {Default 5 ens}
PO	Page offset. {Default 26/27 inches}
PS	Point size. {Default 10 point}
QI	Quotation indent. {Default 5 ens}
VS	Vertical line spacing. {Default 12 point}

Reserved Macro and String Names

The following macro and string names are used by the **ms** package. Avoid using these names for compatibility with the existing macros. An italicized *n* means that the name contains a numeral (generally the interpolated value of a number register).

,	.]	:	[.	[c	[o	^	'	~
1C	2C	AB	AE	AI	A*n*	AT	AU	AX
B	B1	B2	BB	BG	BT	BX	C	C1
C2	CA	CC	CF	CH	CM	CT	DA	DW
DY	EE	EG	EL	EM	EN	E*n*	EQ	EZ
FA	FE	FF	FG	FJ	FK	FL	FN	FO
FS	FV	FX	FY	HO	I	IE	IH	IM
I*n*	IP	IZ	KD	KF	KJ	KS	LB	LG
LP	LT	MC	ME	MF	MH	MN	MO	MR
ND	NH	NL	NP	OD	OK	PP	PT	PY
QE	QF	QP	QS	R	R3	RA	RC	RE
R*n*	RP	RS	RT	S0	S2	S3	SG	SH
SM	SN	SY	TA	TC	TD	TE	TH	TL
TM	TQ	TR	TS	TT	TX	UL	US	UX
WB	WH	WT	XF	XK	XP			

-ms Macros

Reserved Number Register Names

The following number register names are used by the ms package. An italicized n means that the name contains a numeral (generally the interpolated value of another number register).

nT	AJ	AV	BC	BD	BE	BH	BI	BQ
BW	CW	EF	FC	FL	FM	FP	GA	GW
H1	H2	H3	H4	H5	HM	HT	I0	IF
IK	IM	IP	IR	IS	IT	IX	In	Jn
KG	KI	KM	L1	LE	LL	LT	MC	MF
MG	ML	MM	MN	NA	NC	ND	NQ	NS
NX	OJ	PD	PE	PF	PI	PN	PO	PQ
PS	PX	QI	QP	RO	SJ	ST	T.	TB
TC	TD	TK	TN	TQ	TV	TY	TZ	VS
WF	XX	YE	YY	ZN				

Note that with the exception of [c and [o, none of the number register, macro, or string names contain lowercase letters, so lower or mixed case names are a safe bet when you're writing your own macros.

-me Macros

.1c	**.1c** Return to single-column format. (See **.2c**.)
.2c	**.2c** Enter two-column format. Force a new column with **.bc**; end two-column mode with **.1c**.
.ar	**.ar** Set page number in Arabic.
.b	**.b** *w x* Set *w* in bold and *x* in previous font (underline in *nroff*).

.(b	**.(b** *type*
	
	Begin block keep. End with **.)b**.
	
	type
	   C centered block keep
	   F filled block keep
	   L left-justified block keep

.)b	**.)b** End block keep. (See **.(b**).

.ba _n_   **.ba**

Set the base indent to _n_.

.bc   **.bc**

Begin column (used after **.2c**).

.bi _w x_   **.bi**

Set _w_ in bold italics and _x_ in previous font.

.bl _n_   **.bl**

Leave _n_ contiguous white space. Equivalent to **.sp** _n_ inside a block.

.bx _w x_   **.bx**

Set _w_ in a box and _x_ immediately outside the box.

.+c _title_   **.+c**

Begin chapter with _title_.

.$c _title_   **.$c**

Begin numbered chapter with _title_.

.$C _keyword n title_   **.$C**

User-definable macro. Called by **.$c**, supplying _keyword_ (e.g., "Chapter" or "Appendix"); chapter or

☞

Macros

.$C *continued*	appendix number (*n*), and *title*.
.(c	**.(c** Begin centered block. End with **.)c**.
.)c	**.)c** End centered block.
.(d	**.(d** Begin delayed text. End with **.)d**.
.)d	**.)d** End delayed text. Print text with **.pd**.
.ef	**.ef** '*l*'*c*'*r*' Print three-part footer on all *even* pages. Parts are left-justified, centered and right-justified at bottom of every even page.
.eh	**.eh** '*l*'*c*'*r*' Print three-part heading on all *even* pages. Parts are left-justified, centered and right-justified at top of every even page.
.ep	**.ep** End this page and print footnotes.

.EN

.EN

End equation. (See **.EQ**).

.EQ *type title*

.EQ

Begin equation to be processed by *eqn* of specified
type, and with specified *title* printed on the right margin next to the equation. End with **.EN**. See Section
7 for more information on *eqn*.

type

C	centered.
I	indented.
L	left justified.

.$f

.$f

Call to print footer.

.(f

.(f

Begin text for footnote. End with **.)f**.

.)f

.)f

End of footnote text.

.fo *'l'c'r'*

.fo

Print three-part footer on *all* pages. Parts are left-
justified, centered and right-justified at bottom of
every page.

.$H	**.$H** Normally undefined macro, called immediately before printing text on a page. Can be used for column headings, etc.
.$h	**.$h** Call to print header.
.he	**.he** '*l*'*c*'*r*' Print three-part heading on *all* pages. Parts are left-justified, centered and right-justified at top of every page.
.hl	**.hl** Draw a horizontal line length of page.
.hx	**.hx** Do not print headings and footers on next page.
.i	**.i** *w x* Set *w* in italics and *x* in previous font (underline in *nroff*).
.ip	**.ip** *label n* Indent paragraph *n* spaces with hanging label.

.ix [±*n*] Indent, no break. Equivalent to **'in** *n*.	**.ix**

.(l *type*
 	
Begin list. End with **.)l**.
type
   C   centered list
   F   filled list
   L   left-justified list
	.(l

.)l End list. (See **.(l**).	**.)l**
.ll +*n* Set line length to +*n* (all environments).	**.ll**
.lo Loads another set of macros which is intended to be a set of locally defined macros.	**.lo**
.lp Begin block paragraph (left-justified).	**.lp**
.m1 *n* Set *n* spaces between top of page and heading.	**.m1**

Macros

.m2	**.m2** *n* Set *n* spaces between heading and first line of text.
.m3	**.m3** *n* Set *n* spaces between footer and text.
.m4	**.m4** *n* Set *n* spaces between footer and bottom of page.
.n1	**.n1** Number lines in margin beginning with 1.
.n2*n*	**.n2***n* Number lines in margin beginning with *n*; stop numbering if *n* is 0.
.np	**.np** Numbered paragraphs.
.of	**.of** '*l*'*c*'*r*' Print three-part footer on *all* odd pages. Parts are left-justified, centered and right-justified at bottom of every odd page.

.oh '*l*'*c*'*r*'

.oh

Print three-part heading on *all* odd pages. Parts are left-justified, centered and right-justified at top of every odd page.

.$p *title n d*

.$p

Print section heading with specified *title*, section number n, and depth of section d.

.$0 *title n d*

.$0

Called automatically after every call to **.$p**. Normally undefined, but may be used to automatically put every section title into table of contents, or for some similar function.

.$1-.$6

.$1-.$6

Traps called just before printing that depth section. These macros are called from **.$p**.

.pa [±*n*]

.pa

Equivalent to **.bp**.

.pd

.pd

Print delayed text (indicated by **.(d** and **.)d**).

.pp

.pp

Begin indented paragraph.

.q	**.q** *w x* Surround *w* with double quotes and *x* immediately outside quotes.
.(q	**.(q** Begin major quote. End with **.)q**.
.)q	**.)q** End major quote.
.r	**.r** *w x* Set *w* in Roman font and *x* in previous font.
.rb	**.rb** *w x* Set *w* in bold and *x* in previous font.
.re	**.re** Reset tabs to every 0.5 inches in *troff* and every 0.8 inch in *nroff*.
.ro	**.ro** Set page number in Roman numerals.
.$s	**.$s** Separate footnotes with 1.5-inch horizontal line.

.sh Begin numbered section heading.	**.sh**
.sk Leave next page blank.	**.sk**
.sx +*n* Begin a paragraph at level *n*.	**.sx**
.sz *n* Set character point size to *n* (line spacing set proportionally).	**.sz**
.th Initialize for a thesis.	**.th**
.tp Initialize for a title page.	**.tp**
.TS [H] Start table. End with **.TE**. See Section 7 for more information on *tbl*. **H** put table header on all pages. End entry of table header with **.TH**.	**.TS**

Macros

.TH	**.TH** Table header ends. Must be used with **.TS H**.
.TE	**.TE** End table. (See **.TS**).
.u	**.u** *w x* Underline *w* and set *x* in previous font.
.uh	**.uh** *title* Begin unnumbered section heading using *title*.
.(x	**.(x** Begin index entry.
.)x	**.)x** End index entry. Print with **.xp**.
.)x_	**.)x_** No page number for index.
.x1	**.x1** *n* Set the line length to *n* (current environment only).

.xp

Print index. (See .(x).

.xp

.(z

Begin floating keep.

.(z

.)z

End floating keep.

.)z

.++ type header

Defines the section of the paper being entered.

.++

Macros

Preprocessors

This section is divided into three subsections, each covering a different preprocessor of the *nroff/troff* formatting system. These sections are:

- The *tbl* preprocessor.
- The *eqn* preprocessor.
- The *pic* graphics language.

See Section 1 for command line options for the various commands.

Each of these preprocessors translate code into *nroff/troff* requests and escape sequences; run independently of the formatter, they can be used to confirm that syntax is correct, or to determine where it fails. For example, to run *tbl* alone on the command line, use the command,

tbl *file*

tbl

The success of a table to be processed by *tbl* depends largely on the header lines, which consist of one line listing the options and one or more format lines. Each field of the table input must be separated by a tab or designated tab symbol, with each row input entirely on a single line unless a field is enclosed by "T{" and "T}".

tbl Macros

.TS	Start table.
.TE	End table.
.TS H	Used when the table will continue onto more than one page. Used with .TH to define a header that will print on every page.
.TH	With .TS H, ends the header portion of the table.
.T&	Continue table after changing format line.

Options

Options affect the entire table. The options should be separated by commas, and the option line must be terminated by a semicolon.

center	Center with *current* margins.
expand	Flush with current right *and* left margins.
(blank)	Flush with current left margin (Default).
box	Enclose table in a box.
doublebox	Enclose table in two boxes.
allbox	Enclose each table entry in a box.
tab (*x*)	Define the tab symbol as *x*.
linesize *n*	Set lines or rules (e.g., from box) to *n* point type.
delim *xy*	Recognize *x* and *y* as the *eqn* delimiters.

The format line affects the layout of individual columns and rows of the table. Each line contains a key letter for each column of the table. The column entries should be separated by spaces, and the format section must be terminated by a period. Each line of format corresponds to one line of the table, except for the last, which corresponds to all following lines up to the next .T&, if any.

Key letters:

c	Center.
l	Left justify.
r	Right justify.
n	Align numerical entries.
a	Align alphabetic subcolumns.
s	Horizontally span previous column entry across this column.
^	Vertically continue entry from previous row down through this row.

Other options (must follow a key letter):

b	Boldface.
i	Italics.
fx	Font x.
pn	Point size.
t	Begin any corresponding vertically spanned table entry at the top line of its range.
e	Equal width columns.
w(n)	Minimum column width. Also used with text blocks. n can be given in any acceptable *troff* units.
vn	Vertical line spacing. Used *only* with text blocks.
n	Amount of separation between columns {Default is 3n}.
|	Single vertical line. Typed between key letters.
||	Double vertical line. Typed between key letters.
_	Single horizontal line. Used in place of a key letter.
=	Double horizontal line. Used in place of a key letter.

The data portion includes both the heading and text of the table. Each table entry must be separated by a tab symbol.

.xx	*troff* requests may be used (such as .sp #, .ce #, etc.).
\	As last character in a line, combine following line with current line (hide newline).
\^	Vertically spanned table entry. Span table entry immediately above down over this row.
_ or =	As the only character in a line, extend a single or double horizontal line the full width of the table.
\$_ or \$=	Extend a single or double horizontal line the full width of the column.
_	Extend a single horizontal line the width of the *contents* of the column.
\R*x*	Print *x*'s as wide as the *contents* of the column.
... [*tab*]T{	Start text block as a table entry. Must end a line. Necessary when a line of text is input over more than one line, or will span more than one line of output.
... T}[*tab*]	End text block. Must begin a line.

A tbl Example

Input:

```
.TS
center,box,linesize (6),tab(@);
cb s s.
Horizontal Local Motions
_
.T&
ci | ci s
ci | ci s
ci | ci | ci
c | l s.
Function@Effect in
\^@_
\^@troff@nroff
_
\eh'n'@Move distance N
\e(space)@Unpaddable space-size space
\e0@Digit-size space
_
.T&
c | l | l.
\e|@1/6 em space@ignored
\e^@1/12 em space@ignored
.TE
```

Result:

Horizontal Local Motions		
Function	*Effect in*	
	troff	*nroff*
\h'n'	Move distance N	
\(space)	Unpaddable space-size space	
\0	Digit-size space	
\\|	1/6 em space	ignored
\^	1/12 em space	ignored

eqn is a preprocessor designed to facilitate the typesetting of mathematical equations.

.EQ	Start Typesetting Mathematics.
.EN	End Typesetting Mathematics.

Character Translations

The character sequences below are recognized and translated as shown.

Char	Trans	Char	Trans
>=	$\geq$	approx	$\approx$
<=	$\leq$	nothing	
==	$\equiv$	cdot	$\cdot$
!=	$\neq$	times	$\times$
+-	$\pm$	del	∇
->	$\rightarrow$	grad	∇
<-	$\leftarrow$	...	$\cdots$
<<	$\ll$	,...,	$, \cdots ,$
>>	$\gg$	sum	$\sum$
inf	∞	int	$\int$
partial	∂	prod	$\prod$
half	$\frac{1}{2}$	union	$\cup$
prime	$'$	inter	$\cap$

Digits, parenthesis, brackets, punctuation marks, and the following words are converted to Roman font when encountered:

> sin cos tan sinh cosh tanh
> arc max min lin log ln
> exp Re Im and if for det

Greek letters can be printed in upper or lower case. To obtain Greek letters, simply spell them out:

Char	Trans	Char	Trans
alpha	α	tau	τ
beta	β	upsilon	υ
gamma	γ	phi	ϕ
delta	δ	chi	χ
epsilon	ε	psi	ψ
zeta	ζ	omega	ω
eta	η	GAMMA	Γ
theta	θ	DELTA	Δ
iota	ι	THETA	Θ
kappa	κ	LAMBDA	Λ
lambda	λ	XI	Ξ
mu	μ	PI	Π
nu	ν	SIGMA	Σ
xi	ξ	UPSILON	Y
omicron	o	PHI	Φ
pi	π	PSI	Ψ
rho	ρ	OMEGA	Ω
sigma	σ		

The following words translate to marks on the tops of characters.

Char	Trans
x dot	$\dot{x}$
x dotdot	$\ddot{x}$
x hat	$\hat{x}$
x tilde	$\tilde{x}$
x vec	$\vec{x}$
x dyad	$\overleftrightarrow{x}$
x bar	$\bar{x}$
x under	$\underline{x}$

——Words Recognized by eqn

above   Separate the pieces of a pile or matrix column.

back *n*   Move backwards horizontally *n* 1/100's of an 'm'.

bold   Change to bold font.

ccol   Center align a column of a matrix.

col???	Used with a preceding r or l to left or right adjust the columns of the matrix.
cpile	Make a centered pile (same as pile).
define	Create a name for a frequently used string.
delim	Define two characters to mark the left and right ends of an EQN equation to be printed in line.
down n	Move down n 1/100's of an 'm'.
fat	Widen the current font by overstriking it.
font x	Change to font x where x is the one character name or the number of a font.
from	Used in Summations, Integrals and similar constructions to signify the lower limit.
fwd n	Move forwards horizontally n 1/100's of an 'm'.
gfont x	Set a global font x for all equations.
gsize n	Set a global size for all equations.
up n	Move up n 1/100's of an 'm'.
italic	Change to italic font.
lcol	Left justify a column of a matrix.
left	Create big brackets, big braces, big bars, etc.
lineup	Line up marks in equations on different lines.
lpile	Left justify the elements of a pile.
mark	Remember the horizontal position in an equation. Used with lineup.
matrix	Create a matrix.
ndefine	Create a definition which only takes effect when NEQN is running.
over	Make a fraction.
pile	Make a vertical pile with elements centered above one another.
rcol	Right adjust a column of a matrix.
right	Create big brackets, big braces, big bars, etc.
roman	Change to Roman font.
rpile	Right justify the elements of a pile.
size n	Change the size of the font to n.
sqrt	Draw a square root sign.
sub	Start a subscript.
sup	Start a superscript.
tdefine	Make a definition which will apply only for EQN.

to	Used in Summations, Integrals and similar constructions to signify the upper limit.
~	Force extra space into the output.
^	Force a space one half the size of the space forced by ~ .
{ }	Force EQN to treat an element as a unit.
'...'	A string within quotes is not subject to alterations by EQN.

Precedence

If you don't use braces, EQN will do operations in the order shown in this list, reading from left to right.

dyad	*vec*	*under*	*bar*
tilde	*hat*	*dot*	*dotdot*
fwd	*back*	*down*	*up*
fat	*roman*	*italic*	*bold*
size	*sub*	*sup*	*sqrt*
over	*from*	*to*	

These operations group to the left:

over sqrt left right

All others group to the right.

──An eqn Example─────────────────────────────

Input:

```
.EQ
delim %%
.EN
%sum from i=0 to inf c sup i~=~lim from {m -> inf}
sum from i=0 to m c sup i%
```

Result:

$$\sum_{i=0}^{\infty} c^i = \lim_{m \to \infty} \sum_{i=0}^{m} c^i$$

pic

In **pic** there are often dozens of ways to draw a picture, not only because of the many permissible abbreviations, but because it tries to combine the language of geometry with English. You can specify a line, for example, with direction, magnitude, and starting point, yet often achieve the same effect by simply stating, "from *there* to *there*."

Full descriptions of primitive objects in **pic** can be ended by starting another line, or by the semi-colon character (";"). A single primitive description can be continued on the next line, however, by ending the first with a backslash character ("\"). Comments may be placed on lines beginning with "#".

pic Macros

.PS [*h* [*w*]]	Start **pic** description. *h* and *w*, if specified, are the desired height and width of the picture; the full picture will be made to expand or contract to fill this space.
.PS <*file*	Read contents of *file* in place of current line.
.PE	End **pic** description.
.PF	End **pic** description and return to vertical position before matching **PS**.
.xx	*troff* request (or macro) *xx*.

Declarations

At the beginning of a **pic** description, you may declare a new scale, and declare any number of variables.

pic assumes you want a 1-to-1 scale, with 1 = one inch. You can declare a different scale, say 1 = one-*n*th of an inch, by declaring,

    scale = *n*

pic takes variable substitutions for numbers used in the description. Instead of specifying, "**line right** *n*", you may use a lower-case character as a variable, for example "**a**", by declaring at the top of the description:

    a = *n*

You may then write "**line right a**".

Primitives

Primitives may be followed by relevant options. Options are discussed later in this section.

arc [cw] [*options*] ["*text*"]

 A fraction of a circle {Default = 1/4 of a circle}. The **cw** option specifies a clockwise arc; default is counter-clockwise.

arrow [*options*] ["*text*"] [*then*...]

 Draw an arrow. Essentially the same as **line ->**.

box [*options*] ["*text*"]

 Draw a box.

circle [*options*] ["*text*"]

 Draw a circle.

ellipse [*options*] ["*text*"]

 Draw an ellipse.

line [*options*] ["*text*"] [*then*...]

 Draw a line.

move [*options*] ["*text*"]

 A move of position in the drawing. (Essentially, an invisible line).

spline [*options*] ["*text*"] [then...]

 A line, with the feature that a "then" results in a gradual (sloped) change in direction.

"*text***"**

 Text centered at current point.

Options

right [*n*] **left** [*n*] **up** [*n*] **down** [*n*]	Specifies direction of primitive; default is direction in which the previous description had been heading. Diagonals result by using two directions on the option line. Each direction can be followed by a specified length *n*.
rad *n* **diam** *n*	Specifies a primitive to have radius *n* (or diameter *n*).
ht *n* **wld** *n*	Specifies the height or width of the primitive to be *n*. For an arrow, line, or spline, refers to size of arrowhead.
same	Specifies a primitive of the same dimensions of the most recent matching primitive.
at *point*	Specifies primitive to be centered at *point*.

with *.position* **at** *point*

> Specifies the designated *position* of the primitive to be at *point*.

from *point1* **to** *point2*

> Specifies the primitive to be drawn from *point1* to *point2*.

Points may be expressed as Cartesian coordinates or in respect to previous objects.

->	Specify the arrowhead to be directed forwards.
<-	Specify the arrowhead to be directed backwards.
<->	Specify the arrowhead to be directed both ways.

chop *n m*   Chop off *n* from beginning of primitive, and *m* from end. With only one argument, the same value will be chopped from both ends.

dotted
dashed   Specifies the primitive to be drawn dotted, dashed, or to be invisible. Default is solid line.
invis

then ...   Continue primitive in a new direction. Relevant only to lines, splines, moves, and arrows.

Text

Text is be placed within quotes. To break the line, break into two (or more) sets of quotes.

Text always appears centered within the object, unless given one of the following arguments:

ljust	Text appears left-justified to the center.
rjust	Text appears right-justified to the center.
above	Text appears above the center.
below	Text appears below the center.

Object Blocks

A complex object which is the combination of several primitives (for example, an octagon) can be treated as a single object by declaring it as a block:

Object: [
   description

   .

   .

   .

   ]

Brackets are used as delimiters. Note that the object is declared as a proper noun, hence should begin with a capital letter.

Macros

The same sequence of commands can be repeated by using macros. The syntax is:

define *sequence* %
   description

   .

   .

   .

   %

Here we have used the percent sign ("%") as the delimiter, but any character which is not in the description may be used.

Macros can take variables, expressed in the definition as "$1" through "$9". Invoke the macro with the syntax:

   sequence(value1,value2, . . .)

Positioning

In a **pic** description, the first action will begin at (0,0), unless otherwise specified with coordinates. Thus, the point (0,0) will move down and right on the drawing, as objects are placed above and left of the first object.

All points are ultimately translated by the formatter into x- and y-coordinates. You may therefore refer to a specific point in the picture by incrementing or decrementing by coordinates, i.e., "**2nd ellipse - (3,1)**".

You may refer to the x- and y coordinates of an object by placing "**.x**" or "**.y**" at the end, for example, "**last box.x**" will refer to the x-coordinate of the most recent box drawn. Some of the physical attributes of the object may also be referred to similarly, as follows:

.x	x-coordinate of object's center
.y	y-coordinate of object's center
.ht	height of object
.wid	width of object
.rad	radius of object

Unless otherwise positioned, each object will begin at the point where the last object left off. If a command (or sequence of commands) is set off by curly braces ("{", "}"), however, pic will then return to the point before the first brace.

Positioning Between Objects

When referring to a previous object, you must use proper names. This can be done two ways:

1. By referring to it by order, e.g., 1st box, 3rd box, last box, 2nd last box, etc.

2. By declaring it with a name, in initial caps, on its declaration line, e.g.,

    Line1: line 1.5 right from last box.sw

To refer to a point between two objects, or between two points on the same object, you may write:

fraction **of the way between** *first.position* **and** *second.position*

or (abbreviated):

fraction<first.position,second.position>

Corners

When you refer to a previous object, pic will assume that you mean the *center* of the object, unless you use a *corner* to specify a particular point on the object. The syntax used is:

.corner **of** *object*

(for example, "**.sw of last box**"), or (abbreviated):

object.corner

(for example, "**last box.sw**").

These corners may be:

n	north (same as "top")
s	south (same as "bottom")
e	east (same as "right")
w	west (same as "left")
ne	northeast
nw	northwest
se	southeast
sw	southwest
t	top (same as "north")
b	bottom (same as "south")
r	right (same as "east")
l	left (same as "west")
start	point where drawing of object began
end	point where drawing of object ended

You may also refer to the **upper right**, **upper** left, lower right, and lower **left** of an object.

Numerical Operators

Several operators are functional in **pic**. These are:

+	addition
−	subtraction
*	multiplication
/	divided by
%	modulo

Default Values

arcrad	0.25	**ellipsewid**	0.75
arrowwid	0.05	**linewid**	0.5
arrowht	0.1	**lineht**	0.5
boxwid	0.75	**movewid**	0.5
boxht	0.5	**moveht**	0.5
circlerad	0.25	**scale**	1
dashwid	0.05	**textht**	0
ellipseht	0.5	**textwid**	0

Input:

```
.PS
define smile %
a = $1
circle radius a at 0,0
arc cw radius a*.75 from a*.5,-a*.25 to -a*.5,-a*.25
"\(bu" at a*.33,a*.25
"\(bu" at a*-.33,a*.25
%
smile(.5)
.PE
```

Result:

8

Program Debugging

This section covers the debugging programs provided for the UNIX environment: **adb** (absolute **debugger**), **sdb** (symbolic **debugger**) and **dbx**. These programs take an executable object file and its corefile, the core image file produced when *objfile* is executed. These debugging programs then provide a controlled environment for the execution of the program.

If *objfile* and *corefile* are not specified, **a.out** is taken as the default object file and **core** as the default core image file.

The adb Debugging Program

adb [-w] [*objfile*] [*corefile*]

-w   Create both *objfile* and *corefile* if necessary, making them read-write for **adb**.

Requests to **adb** are read from the standard input, of the general form:

[*address*] [, *count*] [*command*] [;]

The *dot* variable is set to *address* if it is specified; its default value is 0. *count* specifies how many times the command will be executed.

address and *count* are expressions of one of the forms described below.

Expressions

Expression	Value
.	The value of *dot*.
+	The value of *dot*, plus the current increment.
-	The value of *dot*, minus the current increment.
"	The most recent *address*.
int	A decimal number, unless it begins with:
	0 Octal number.
	# Hexadecimal number.
int.frac	A 32-bit floating point number.
'cccc'	ASCII value of up to 4 characters.
<x	The value of *x*.
symbol	A sequence of characters, not starting with a digit.
(exp)	The value of *exp*.

Monadic Operators:

@	Contents of address in *objfile*.
*	Contents of address in *corefile*.
−	Integer negation.
~	Bitwise complement.

Dyadic Operators:

+	Addition.
-	Subtraction.
*	Multiplication.
%	Integer division.
&	Bitwise and.
|	Bitwise or.
#	Round up to next multiple.

Addresses

Addresses are interpreted according to the context in which they are used. A mapping from a written address to the file determines the file address. If the triples $(b1, e1, f1)$ and $(b2, e2, f2)$ represent the mapping for that file, the written address is calculated by the formula:

$$b1 \leq address < e1 => file\ address = address + f1 - b1$$

or,

$$b2 \leq address < e2 => file\ address = address + f2 - b2$$

Commands

Formatted Printing:

Command	Function
?*format*	Print from *objfile* according to *format*.
/*format*	Print from *corefile* according to *format*.
=*format*	Print the value of *dot* (current address).
[/?]l *expr mask*	Locate *expr* from *objfile* or *corefile* words masked with *mask*.
[/?]w *expr*	Write *expr* into *objfile* or *corefile*.

Breakpoint and Program Control:

Command	Function
:b*c*	Set breakpoint at *dot* and execute command *c*.
:c*s*	Continue running program with signal *s*.
:d	Delete breakpoint.
:k	Kill the program being debugged.
:r	Run *objfile* under **adb** control.
:s*s*	Single step with signal *s*.

Miscellaneous Commands:

Command	Function
[?/]m *bl el fl*[?/]	Record new values for (*bl*, *el*, *fl*).
!*cmd*	Execute the command *cmd*.
>*name*	Assign *dot* to variable or register *name*.
$b	Print current breakpoints.
$c	C stack trace.
$d	Reset integer input to the default.
$e	External variables.
$<*f*	Read commands from file *f*.
$>*f*	Send output to file *f*.
$m	Print the address map.
$o	Treat input integers as octal.
$q	Exit from **adb**.
$r	General registers.
$s	Set offset for symbol match.
$v	Print **adb** variables in octal.
$w	Set output line width.

Format Summary

If no format is given in a command, the most recent format is used. *Format* consists of one or more characters specifying a style of printing. A decimal integer may precede each character, as a repeat count for the character. The *dot* variable is incremented by the amount given for each format character.

Character	Significance
a	The value of dot.
b	One byte in octal.
c	One byte as a character.
C	One byte as a character with 000 to 040 printed as @.
d	One word in decimal.
D	Long in decimal.
f	Two words in floating point.
F	Double in floating point.
i	Assembly instructions.
o	One word in octal.
O	Two words in octal.
q	Signed octal.
Q	Long signed octal.
p	The addressed value in symbolic form.
n	A newline.
r	A blank space.
s	A null terminated character string.
S	A string using the @ escape convention.
*n*t	Move to next *n* space tab.
u	One word as unsigned integer.
U	Long unsigned integer.
x	2 bytes in hexadecimal.
X	4 bytes in hexadecimal.
Y	Date.
^	Backup *dot*.
" ... "	Print the enclosed string.

Variables

Named variables are set initially by **adb** but are not used. Numbered variables are used as follows:

Variable	Value
0	The last value printed.
1	The last offset part of an instruction source.
2	The previous value of variable 1.

The system header in *corefile* sets the following variables on entry to **adb**:

Variable	Value
b	The base address of the data segment.
d	The data segment size.
e	The entry point.
m	The "magic" number.
s	The stack segment size.
t	The text segment size.

The adb Debugging Program

The sdb Debugging Program

sdb [-w] [-W] [*objfile* [*corefile* [*dir*]]]
    -w   overwrite locations in **objfile**.
    -W   do not warn if source files older than *objfile* cannot be found.

a "-" in place of *corefile* will force **sdb** to ignore any core image file.

sdb can be used to debug programs written in the C and F77 languages.

Commands

Formatted Printing:

t	Print a stack trace.
T	Print the top line of the stack trace.
variable/clm	Print variable according to length *l* and format *m*:

        l: **b**   One byte.
             h   Two bytes.
             l   Four bytes.

        m: **a**   Characters starting at variable's address.
             c   Character.
             d   Decimal.
             f   32-bit floating.
             g   64-bit double precision floating.
             i   Machine language instruction.
             I   Machine language instruction with numerical address.
             o   Octal.
             p   Pointer to procedure.
             s   Print characters starting at address pointed to by variable.
             u   Unsigned decimal.
             x   Hexadecimal.

linenumber?lm *variable:?lm*	Print from **a.out** and procedure *variable* according to length *l* and format *m*.
variable=lm *linenumber=lm* *number=lm*	Print the address of *variable* or *linenumber*, in the format specified by *l* and *m*. Use the last form to convert *number* to the format specified by *l* and *m*.
variable!value	Assign *value* to *variable*.
x	Display the machine registers and the machine instructions.
X	Display the machine instructions.

Examining the Source:

Command	Function
e *name*	Set the procedure, file, or directory name.
p	Display the current line.
z	Display the current line and several following lines.
w	Display the lines around the current line.
/*regular expression*/	Search ahead for the specified *regular expression*.
?*regular expression*?	Search back for the specified *regular expression*.
number	Make *number* the current line.
count+	Advance *count* lines.
count-	Go back *count* lines.

Executing the Source:

Command	Function
count r *args*	Run the program with the specified arguments. Ignore *count* breakpoints.
count R	Run the program with the no arguments. Ignore *count* breakpoints.
level v	Verbose mode toggle. *level* values 1= source level, 2= assembler level.
linenumber a	Set a breakpoint at *linenumber* and inform the user.
linenumber b *commands*	Set breakpoint at *linenumber* and optionally execute command at breakpoint.
linenumber c *count*	Continue after a breakpoint or ignore *count* breakpoints then stop. If *linenumber* is specified set a temporary breakpoint at *linenumber*.
linenumber C *count*	Continue after a breakpoint (with the halt signal reactivated) or ignore *count* breakpoints then stop. If *linenumber* is specified set a temporary breakpoint at *linenumber*.
linenumber d	Delete breakpoint at *linenumber*.
linenumber g *count*	Continue at *linenumber* after a breakpoint.
procedure (arg1,arg2, . . .)	Execute *procedure*.
procedure (arg1,arg2, . . .)/m	Execute procedure and print result in format *m*.
variable$m *count*	Single step until *variable* is modified.

Miscellaneous Commands:

Command	Function
!cmd	Execute *cmd* with *sh*.
Newline	Display the next line or memory location.
CTRL-D	Scroll the display.
<*file*	Execute the commands contained in *file*.
string	Print *string*.

Breakpoint and Program Control

Command	Function
B	Display the active breakpoints.
D	Remove all breakpoints.
i	Single step mode.
I	Single step with the halt signal activated.
k	Kill the program.
l	Display the last line executed.
M	Display the address map.
M [?/][*]*b e f*	Record new values for the address map.
q	Exit.
s*count*	Single step *count* lines.
S*count*	Single step *count* procedures.
address:m*count*	Single step until *address* is modified.

Debugging the Debugger:

Command	Function
V	Display the version number.
Q	Display a list of procedures and files being debugged.
Y	Toggle debug output.

Debugging

The dbx Debugging Program

dbx [*options*] [*objfile* [*corefile*]]

-i   force standard input terminal or terminal emulator type function.
-I*dir*   add *dir* to the directory search path.
-k   use Kernel debug mode.
-r   execute *objfile* without waiting.
-c*file* execute **dbx** commands from *file* before reading standard input.

dbx can be used to debug programs in the C, FORTRAN, and PASCAL languages.

Commands

Execution and Tracing:

run [*args*] [<*file1*] [>*file2*] **rerun** [*args*] [<*file1*] [>*file2*]	Begin executing *objfile*, with command line arguments *args*. **rerun** without arguments will run program with same arguments as previous **run** or **rerun**.
trace [*trace*] [**if** *cond*]	Print tracing information as program is executed. With no arguments, all source lines are printed before being executed. *trace* can be:
n	print line *n* of the source before it is executed.
in *funct* *funct1* [**in** *funct2*]	print information about the named procedure or function every time it is invoked.
expr	print value of *expr* each time line *n* is reached. If first argument is a variable *var*, its value is printed each time it is redefined.
var [**in** *funct*]	print value of *var* each time it is redefined.

The "**in** *funct*" condition restricts information from being printed except while executing from within the specified procedure or function.

stop *restriction*	Stop execution when specified *restriction* is true. *restriction* may be:
	    if *condition*
	    at *n* [**if** *condition*]
	    in *funct* [**if** *condition*]
	    var [**if** *condition*]

status [> *file*]	Print out active **trace** and **stop** commands.
delete *n*	Remove traces and stops corresponding to given command numbers, given by **status**.
catch *arg* **ignore** *arg*	Start or stop trapping a signal before it is sent to the program. Specify the signals by number *n* or by name *sig*.
cont *sig*	Continue execution from the point at which it was stopped. If a signal name or number is specified, continue as if it had received the signal.
step	Execute one source line.
next	Execute up to next source line (will not stop before executing procedure or function call).
return [*procedure*]	Continue until a return to *procedure* (or current procedure) is called.
call *funct(parameters)*	Execute object code associated with named procedure or function.

Printing Variables and Expressions:

assign *var* = *expr*	Assign variable *var* the value of *expr*.
dump [*procedure*] [> *file*]	Print names and values of variables in given procedure (or in current procedure with no arguments). All active variables dumped with ".".
print *expr1* [, *expr2* ...]	Print the values of given expressions.
whatis *name*	Print declaration of given *name*.
which *id*	Print the qualification of given identifier *id*.
up [*n*] **down** [*n*]	Move current function up or down stack *n* levels.
where	Print active procedures and functions.
whereis *id*	Print qualification of all symbols with names matching *id*.

Source File Access:

/pattern[/]	Search forward or backward for *pattern*.
?pattern[?]	

edit [*file*] Invoke editor on *file* (or on current source if no ar-
edit *funct* guments are given), or on the file containing given
procedure or function *funct*.

file [*file*] Change current source file name to *file*, or with no
arguments, print current source file name.

func [*funct*] Change current function, or print current function
with no arguments.

list [*nl* [,*n2*]] List the text between lines *nl* and *n2*, or lines sur-
list *funct* rounding the first statement of procedure or function
funct. With no arguments, list the next ten lines.

use *dirs* Search directories *dir* for source files.

Aliases and Variables:

alias *chars string* Define *chars* to a be an alias for *string*.
set *var* [= *expr*] Define value *expr* for variable *var*.
unalias *chars* Remove an alias.
unset *var* Remove a variable.

Machine Commands:

tracei[*address*][**if***condition*]
tracei[*variable*][**at***address*][**if***condition*]
stopi[*address*][**if***condition*]
stopi[**at**][*address*][**if***condition*]
Turn on tracing or set a stop using machine instruction addresses.

stepi
nexti
Same as **step** or **next**, but single instruction instead of source line.

address1, address2/ [*mode*]
address1 / [*n*] [*mode*]
Print contents of memory starting at *address1* up to *address2* or
printing of *n* items. Supported modes are listed below.

Supported Modes:

i   print machine instruction.
d   print a short word in decimal.
D   print a long word in decimal.
o   print a short word in octal.
O   print a long word in octal.
x   print a short word in hexadecimal.
X   print a long word in hexadecimal.
b   print a byte in octal.
c   print a byte as a character.
s   print a string a characters terminated by a null byte.
f   print a single precision real number.
g   print a double precision real number.

Miscellaneous Commands:

gripe	Send a message to user in charge of **dbx**.
help	Print synopsis of **dbx** commands.
quit	Exit **dbx**.
sh *command*	Pass *command* to shell to execute.
source *file*	Read commands for **dbx** from *file*.

9

SCCS and Make

The UNIX operating system earned its reputation above all by providing an unexcelled environment for software development. The **make** and SCCS utilities are widely regarded as the greatest contributors to the efficiency of this environment.

The **make** program performs automatic update of a group of interrelated programs. The SCCS system allows all changes to the source code to be recorded, preventing the confusion that may arise from simply saving multiple versions of a source file.

SCCS

The Source Code Control System (SCCS) makes it possible for a user to keep track of each revision of a document, avoiding the confusion that often arises from having several versions of one file on line. It is particularly useful when enhancements are made to a program, but the original may still be useful to keep around. Each time a file is "entered" into SCCS, SCCS makes note of which lines have been changed or deleted since the most previous version, and from that information can regenerate the file on demand. Each set of changes is dependent on all previous sets of changes.

Each set of changes is called a "delta", and is assigned a SCCS identification string (*sid*). The *sid* consists of either two components, release and level numbers (in the form *a.b*), or of four components: the release, level, branch, and sequence numbers (in the form *a.b.c.d*). The branches and sequences are for situations when two on-running versions of the same file are recorded in SCCS. For example, *delta 3.2.1.1* refers to release 3, level 2, branch 1, sequence 1.

The SCCS file which holds all the changes must be prefixed by "**s.**".

See Section 1 for syntax lines and options for SCCS commands.

Creating a SCCS File

The **admin** command with the -i option creates and initializes SCCS files. For example,

admin -ich01 s.ch01

creates a new SCCS file and initializes it with the contents of **ch01**, which will become *delta 1.1*. The message, "No id keywords (cm7)" appears if you do not specify any keywords. In general, "id keywords" refer to variables in the files that are replaced with appropriate values by **get**, identifying the date and time of creation, the version retrieved, etc. A listing of identification keywords occurs later in this section.

Once the **s.ch01** file is created, the original file **ch01** can be removed, since it can be easily regenerated with the **get** command.

Retrieving a File

The **get** command can retrieve any version of a file from SCCS. Using the example above, you can retrieve **ch01** by entering

get -e s.ch01

and the messages

```
1.1
new delta 1.2
272 lines
```

may appear. This indicates that you are "getting" *delta 1.1,* and the resulting file has 272 lines of text. When the file is reentered into the SCCS file **s.ch01** with the **delta** command, its changes are *delta 1.2.*

The -e option indicates to SCCS that you intend to make more changes to the file and then reenter it into SCCS. Without this option, you will receive the file with read-only permissions. The -e option, besides releasing the file with read-write permissions, also creates a file **p.ch01**, which records information that will be used by SCCS when the file is returned.

───Creating New Releases and Branches───

The -r option to **get** tells SCCS what release and level number you want, but if no level is specified it defaults to the highest level available. With the command

get -r3.2 ch01

delta 3.2 will be the release. However, the command

get -r3 ch01

returns the highest-numbered level in release 3, for example **3.8.** With the -r option omitted, **get** defaults to the highest release, highest level — in other words, the latest version.

When major changes are in store for a file, you may want to begin a new release of the file. You can do that by "getting" the file with the next highest release number. For example, if the latest release of a file is 3.2, and you want to start release 4, enter:

get -e -r4 ch01

You will receive the message,

```
3.2
new delta 4.1
53 lines
```

If you want to make a change to an older version of the same file, you can enter:

get -e -r2.2 ch01

and receive the message:

```
2.2
new delta 2.2.1.1
121 lines
```

You have now created a new branch from the trunk, stemming from version 2.2. Changes in this delta will not affect those in the trunk deltas, i.e., 2.3, 3.1, etc.

Recording Changes

Once changes have been made to the SCCS file, return it to SCCS with the command:

delta s.ch01

You are prompted for comments on the changes. The **delta** command then does its own **get** and compares the new version of the file with the most recent previous version with the **diff** command. It then outputs messages giving the new release number, and how many lines were inserted, deleted, and unchanged.

SCCS Commands

File arguments to SCCS commands can be either filenames or the names of directories; naming a directory will cause all the files in that directory to be processed, with nonapplicable and nonreadable files ignored. If in place of a file argument a "-" is entered, the command will read from standard input for the names of files to be processed, one on each line.

Error messages produced by aborted SCCS commands are of the form

ERROR *filename*: *message* (*code*)

The *code* is useful for using the **help** command to find out what the nature of your error was, by entering, "**help** *code*".

Commands for the administration of SCCS are as follows:

get	Retrieve versions of SCCS files.
delta	Create a new version of an SCCS file (i.e., append a new *delta*).
admin	Create new SCCS files and change their parameters.
prs	Print portions of SCCS files in a specified format.
help	Clarify diagnostic messages.
rmdel	Remove an accidental *delta* from an SCCS file.
cdc	Change the comment associated with a *delta*.
what	Search for all occurrences of the pattern **get** substitutes for %Z%, and print out the following text.
sccsdiff	Show the difference between any two SCCS files.
comb	Combine consecutive deltas into a single delta.
val	Validate a SCCS file.

——Identification Keywords————————————

The following keywords may be used in an SCCS file:

%M%	module name.
%I%	*sid* of the retrieved text.
%R%	release number.
%L%	level number.
%B%	branch number.
%S%	sequence number.
%D%	current date (YY/MM/DD).
%H%	current date (MM/DD/YY).
%T%	current time (HH:MM:SS).
%E%	date newest applied delta was created (YY/MM/DD).
%G%	date newest applied delta was created (MM/DD/YY).
%U%	time newest applied delta was created (HH:MM:SS).
%Y%	module type, as defined by **admin -ft**type.
%F%	SCCS file name.
%P%	fully qualified SCCS file name.
%Q%	the value of *string*, as defined by **admin -fq**string.
%C%	current line number, intended for identifying where error occurred.
%Z%	the string recognized by **what**.
%W%, %A%	shorthand for providing **what** strings for program files.

SCCS/Make

Data Keywords

Data keywords specify which parts of an SCCS file are to be retrieved and output using the -d option of the prs command.

:Dt:	Delta information.	:Z:	what string delimiter.
:DL:	Delta line statistics.	:F:	SCCS file name.
:Li:	lines inserted by delta.	:PN:	SCCS file pathname.
:Ld:	lines deleted by delta.	:MR:	modification numbers
:Lu:	lines unchanged by delta.		for delta.
:DT:	delta type.	:C:	comments for delta.
:I:	SCCS id string (sid).	:UN:	user names.
:R:	release number.	:FL:	flag list.
:L:	level number.	:Y:	module type flag.
:B:	branch number.	:MF:	modification valida-
:S:	sequence number.		tion flag.
:D:	date delta created.	:MP:	modification valida-
:Dy:	year delta created.		tion pgm name.
:Dm:	month delta created.	:KF:	keyword
:Dd:	day delta created.		error/warning flag.
:T:	time delta created.	:BF:	branch flag.
:Th:	hour delta created.	:J:	joint edit flag.
:Tm:	minutes delta created.	:LK:	locked releases.
:Ts:	seconds delta created.	:Q:	user-defined keyword.
:P:	programmer who created delta.	:M:	module name.
		:CB:	ceiling boundary.
:DS:	delta sequence number.	:FB:	floor boundary.
:DP:	predecessor delta sequence number.	:Ds:	default sid.
		:FD:	file descriptive text.
:DI:	sequence number of deltas.	:ND:	null delta flag.
:Dn:	deltas included (sequence number).	:GB:	gotten body.
		:BD:	body.
:Dx:	deltas excluded (sequence number).	:A:	a form of what string.
:Dg:	deltas ignored (sequence number).	:W:	a form of what string.

The **make** program generates a sequence of commands for execution by the UNIX shell. It uses a table of file dependencies input by the programmer, and with this information, can perform updating tasks automatically for the user. It can keep track of the sequence of commands that create certain files, and the list of files that require other files to be current before they can operate efficiently. When a change is made to a program, the **make** command will create the proper files with a minimum of effort.

For a detailed description of **make**, refer to the Nutshell Handbook, *Managing Projects With Make.*

See Section 1 for the syntax and options for **make**.

Internal Macros

$?   The list of components that have been changed more recently than the current target. Can be used only in normal description file entries — not suffix rules.

$@   The name of the current target, except in description file entries for making libraries, where it becomes the library name. Can be used both in normal description file entries and suffix rules.

$<   The name of the current component which has been modified more recently than the current target. Can be used only in suffix rules and the **.DEFAULT:** entry.

$*   The name — without the suffix — of the current component that has been modified more recently than the current target. Can be used only in suffix rules.

$$@   The name of the current target. Can be used only to the right of the colon in dependency lines.

$%   The name of the corresponding **.o** file when the current target is a library module. Can be used both in normal description file entries and suffix rules.

Macro Modifiers

D   The directory portion of any internal macro name except $?. For example, **$(*D), $(<D), $(@D), $$(@D).**

F   The file portion of any internal macro name except $?. For example, **$(*F), $(<F), $(@F), $$(@F).**

SCCS/Make

Macro String Substitution

$(macro:abc=xyz)
> **Evaluates to the current definition of $(macro),** after substituting the string **xyz** for every occurrence of **abc** that occurs either immediately before a blank or tab, or at the end of the macro definition.

Pseudo-Targets

.DEFAULT: Commands associated with this pseudo-target will be executed if a legitimate target must be made but there are no applicable description file entries or suffix rules.

.IGNORE: Ignore error codes. Same as the -l option flag.

.PRECIOUS: Components you specify for this pseudo-target will not be removed when you send a signal (such as interrupt) that aborts **make.**

.SILENT: Execute commands but do not echo them. Same as the -s option flag.

Description File Command Codes

@   Do not echo this command line.

-    Ignore error return from this command.

Sample Default Macros, Suffixes, and Rules

```
EDITOR = /usr/bin/vi
TERM = tvi950ns
SHELL = /bin/csh
PATH = .:/bin:/usr/bin:/usr/fred:/usr/local
LOGNAME = fred
HOME = /usr/fred
GFLAGS =
GET = get
ASFLAGS =
AS = as
FFLAGS =
FC = f77
CFLAGS = -O
CC = cc
LDFLAGS =
LD = ld
LFLAGS =
LEX = lex
YFLAGS =
YACC = yacc
MAKE = make
$ = $
MAKEFLAGS = b
```

```
.h~.h:
     $(GET) $(GFLAGS) -p $< > $*.h

.s~.a:
     $(GET) $(GFLAGS) -p $< > $*.s
     $(AS) $(ASFLAGS) -o $*.o $*.s
     ar rv $@ $*.o
     -rm -f $*.[so]

.r~.a:
     $(GET) $(GFLAGS) -p $< > $*.r
     $(FC) -c $(FFLAGS) $*.r
     ar rv $@ $*.o
     rm -f $*.[ro]

.e~.a:
     $(GET) $(GFLAGS) -p $< > $*.e
     $(FC) -c $(FFLAGS) $*.e
     ar rv $@ $*.o
     rm -f $*.[eo]

.f~.a:
     $(GET) $(GFLAGS) -p $< > $*.f
     $(FC) -c $(FFLAGS) $*.f
     ar rv $@ $*.o
     rm -f $*.[fo]

.r.a:
     $(FC) -c $(FFLAGS) $<
     ar rv $@ $*.o
     rm -f $*.o

.e.a:
     $(FC) -c $(FFLAGS) $<
     ar rv $@ $*.o
     rm -f $*.o

.f.a:
     $(FC) -c $(FFLAGS) $<
     ar rv $@ $*.o
     rm -f $*.o

.c~.a:
     $(GET) $(GFLAGS) -p $< > $*.c
     $(CC) -c $(CFLAGS) $*.c
     ar rv $@ $*.o
     rm -f $*.[co]

.c.a:
     $(CC) -c $(CFLAGS) $<
     ar rv $@ $*.o
     rm -f $*.o
```

```
.l.c:
      $(LEX) $<
      mv lex.yy.c $@

.y~.c:
      $(GET) $(GFLAGS) -p $< > $*.y
      $(YACC) $(YFLAGS) $*.y
      mv y.tab.c $*.c
      -rm -f $*.y

.y.c:
      $(YACC) $(YFLAGS) $<
      mv y.tab.c $@

.l~.o:
      $(GET) $(GFLAGS) -p $< > $*.l
      $(LEX) $(LFLAGS) $*.l
      $(CC) $(CFLAGS) -c lex.yy.c
      rm -f lex.yy.c $*.l
      mv lex.yy.o $*.o

.l.o:
      $(LEX) $(LFLAGS) $<
      $(CC) $(CFLAGS) -c lex.yy.c
      rm lex.yy.c
      mv lex.yy.o $@

.y~.o:
      $(GET) $(GFLAGS) -p $< > $*.y
      $(YACC) $(YFLAGS) $*.y
      $(CC) $(CFLAGS) -c y.tab.c
      rm -f y.tab.c $*.y
      mv y.tab.o $*.o

.y.o:
      $(YACC) $(YFLAGS) $<
      $(CC) $(CFLAGS) -c y.tab.c
      rm y.tab.c
      mv y.tab.o $@

.s~.o:
      $(GET) $(GFLAGS) -p $< > $*.s
      $(AS) $(ASFLAGS) -o $*.o $*.s
      -rm -f $*.s

.s.o:
      $(AS) $(ASFLAGS) -o $@ $<

.r~.o:
      $(GET) $(GFLAGS) -p $< > $*.r
      $(FC) $(FFLAGS) -c $*.r
      -rm -f $*.r
```

```
.e~.e:
     $(GET) $(GFLAGS) -p $< > $*.e

.e~.o:
     $(GET) $(GFLAGS) -p $< > $*.e
     $(FC) $(FFLAGS) -c $*.e
     -rm -f $*.e

.f~.f:
     $(GET) $(GFLAGS) -p $< > $*.f

.f~.o:
     $(GET) $(GFLAGS) -p $< > $*.f
     $(FC) $(FFLAGS) -c $*.f
     -rm -f $*.f

.r.o:
     $(FC) $(FFLAGS) -c $<

.e.o:
     $(FC) $(FFLAGS) -c $<

.f.o:
     $(FC) $(FFLAGS) -c $<

.c~.c:
     $(GET) $(GFLAGS) -p $< > $*.c

.c~.o:
     $(GET) $(GFLAGS) -p $< > $*.c
     $(CC) $(CFLAGS) -c $*.c
     -rm -f $*.c

.c.o:
     $(CC) $(CFLAGS) -c $<

.sh~:
     $(GET) $(GFLAGS) -p $< > $*.sh
     cp $*.sh $*
     -rm -f $*.sh

.sh:
     cp $< $@

.r~:
     $(GET) $(GFLAGS) -p $< > $*.r
     $(FC) -n $(FFLAGS) $*.r -o $*
     -rm -f $*.r

.r:
     $(FC) $(FFLAGS) $(LDFLAGS) $< -o $@

.e~:
     $(GET) $(GFLAGS) -p $< > $*.e
     $(FC) -n $(FFLAGS) $*.e -o $*
```

```
        -rm -f $*.e

.e:
        $(FC) $(FFLAGS) $(LDFLAGS) $< -o $@

.f~:
        $(GET) $(GFLAGS) -p $< > $*.f
        $(FC) -n $(FFLAGS) $*.f -o $*
        -rm -f $*.f

.f:
        $(FC) $(FFLAGS) $(LDFLAGS) $< -o $@

.c~:
        $(GET) $(GFLAGS) -p $< > $*.c
        $(CC) -n $(CFLAGS) $*.c -o $*
        -rm -f $*.c

.c:
        $(CC) $(CFLAGS) $(LDFLAGS) $< -o $@

.SUFFIXES:
        .o   .c   .c~   .f   .f~   .e   .e~   .r   .r~
        .y   .y~   .l   .l~   .s   .s~   .sh   .sh~   .h   .h~
```

Books That Help People Get More Out of Computers

If you want more information about our books, or want to know where to buy them, we're happy to send it.

☐ Send me a free catalog of titles.

☐ What bookstores in my area carry your books (U.S. and Canada only)?

☐ Where can I buy your books outside the U.S. and Canada?

☐ Send me information about consulting services for documentation or programming.

Name _____

Address _____

_____

City _____

State, ZIP _____

Country _____

NAME

COMPANY

ADDRESS

CITY_____ STATE_____ ZIP_____

BUSINESS REPLY MAIL

FIRST CLASS MAIL PERMIT NO. 80 SEBASTOPOL, CA

POSTAGE WILL BE PAID BY ADDRESSEE

O'Reilly & Associates, Inc.

103 Morris Street Suite A
Sebastopol CA 95472-9902

System Performance Tuning

By Mike Loukides

System Performance Tuning answers one of the most fundamental questions you can ask about your computer: "How can I get it to do more work without buying more hardware?" Anyone who has ever used a computer has wished that the system was faster, particularly at times when it was under heavy load.

If your system gets sluggish when you start a big job, if it feels as if you spend hours waiting for remote file access to complete, if your system stops dead when several users are active at the same time, you need to read this book. Some performance problems do require you to buy a bigger or faster computer, but many can be solved simply by making better use of the resources you already have.

336 pages, ISBN 0-937175-60-9

Essential System Administration

By Æleen Frisch

Like any other multi-user system, UNIX requires some care and feeding. *Essential System Administration* tells you how. This book strips away the myth and confusion surrounding this important topic and provides a compact, manageable introduction to the tasks faced by anyone responsible for a UNIX system.

If you use a stand-alone UNIX system, whether it's a PC or a workstation, you know how much you need this book: on these systems the fine line between a user and an administrator has vanished. Either you're both or you're in trouble. If you routinely provide administrative support for a larger shared system or a network of workstations, you will find this book indispensable. Even if you aren't directly responsible for system administration, you will find that understanding basic administrative functions greatly increases your ability to use UNIX effectively.

466 pages
ISBN 0-937175-80-3

COMPUTER
SECURITY
BASICS

Deborah Russell and G. T. Gangemi Sr.
O'Reilly & Associates, Inc.

Practical UNIX Security

By Simson Garfinkel & Gene Spafford

If you are a UNIX system administrator or user who needs to deal with security, you need this book.

Practical UNIX Security describes the issues, approaches, and methods for implementing security measures—spelling out what the varying approaches cost and require in the way of equipment. After presenting UNIX security basics and network security, this guide goes on to suggest how to keep intruders out, how to tell if they've gotten in, how to clean up after them, and even how to prosecute them. Filled with practical scripts, tricks and warnings, *Practical UNIX Security* tells you what you need to know to make your UNIX system as secure as it can be.

"Worried about who's in your Unix system? Losing sleep because someone might be messing with your computer? Having headaches from obscure computer manuals? Then *Practical Unix Security* is for you. This handy book tells you where the holes are and how to cork'em up.

"Moreover, you'll learn about how Unix security really works. Spafford and Garfinkel show you how to tighten up your Unix system without pain. No secrets here—just solid computing advice. "Buy this book and save on aspirin."—Cliff Stoll
512 pages, ISBN 0-937175-72-2

Computer Security Basics

By Deborah Russell & G.T. Gangemi Sr.

There's a lot more consciousness of security today, but not a lot of understanding of what it means and how far it should go. This handbook describes complicated concepts like trusted systems, encryption and mandatory access control in simple terms.

For example, most U.S. government equipment acquisitions now require "Orange Book" (Trusted Computer System Evaluation Criteria) certification. A lot of people have a vague feeling that they ought to know about the Orange Book, but few make the effort to track it down and read it. *Computer Security Basics* contains a more readable introduction to the Orange Book—why it exists, what it contains, and what the different security levels are all about—than any other book or government publication.
464 pages, ISBN 0-937175-71-4

Managing UUCP and Usenet

10th Edition
By Tim O'Reilly & Grace Todino

For all its widespread use, UUCP is one of the most difficult UNIX utilities to master. Poor documentation, cryptic messages, and differences between various implementations make setting up UUCP links a nightmare for many a system administrator.

This handbook is meant for system administrators who want to install and manage the UUCP and Usenet software. It covers HoneyDanBer UUCP as well as standard Version 2 UUCP, with special notes on Xenix. As one reader noted over the Net, "Don't even TRY to install UUCP without it!"

The Tenth Edition of this classic work has been revised and expanded to include descriptions of:

* How to use NNTP (Network News Transfer Protocol) to transfer Usenet news over TCP/IP and other high-speed networks
* How to get DOS versions of UUCP
* How to set up DOS-based laptop computers as travelling UUCP nodes
* How the UUCP 'g' protocol works

368 pages, ISBN 0-937175-93-5

termcap & terminfo

3rd Edition
By John Strang, Linda Mui, & Tim O'Reilly

The *termcap* and *terminfo* databases are UNIX's solution to the difficulty of supporting many terminals without writing special drivers for each terminal. *termcap* (BSD) and *terminfo* (System V) describe the features of hundreds of terminals, together with a library of routines that allow programs to use those capabilities. This book documents hundreds of capabilities and syntax for each, writing and debugging terminal descriptions, and terminal initialization.

"*termcap & terminfo* has been invaluable at explaining what all those strange characters mean in /etc/termcap. The real value of this one would come if I decided to build my own terminal type. I haven't done that, but the book has surely won back its purchase price by helping me add some flashy screen handling to simple shell scripts."
—UNIX Today

270 pages, ISBN 0-937175-22-6

Using UUCP and Usenet

By Grace Todino & Dale Dougherty

Using UUCP shows how to communicate with both UNIX and non-UNIX systems using UUCP and *cu* or *tip*. It also shows how to read news and post your own articles and mail to other Usenet members. This handbook assumes that UUCP and Usenet links to other computer systems have already been established by your system administrator.

While clear enough for a novice, this book is packed with information that even experienced users will find indispensable. Take the mystery out of questions such as why files sent via UUCP don't always end up where you want them, how to find out the status of your file transfer requests, and how to execute programs remotely with *uux*.

210 pages, ISBN 0-937175-10-2

!%@:: A Directory of Electronic Mail Addressing & Networks

2nd Edition
By Donnalyn Frey & Rick Adams

This book is designed to answer the problem of addressing mail to people you've never met, on networks you've never heard of. It includes a general introduction to the concept of e-mail addressing, followed by a detailed reference section, which provides information for over 130 different networks around the world.

For each network, the book shows: general description, address structure and format, architecture, connections to other networks or sites, facilities available to users, contact name and address, cross references to other networks, future plans and the date of update. Appendixes include indexes to second-level domains, network names, country names, country codes, and a description of how Internet addresses are handled by UUCP sites.

If you routinely send e-mail and want concise, up-to-date information on many of the world's networks, this book is for you.

438 pages
ISBN 0-937175-15-3

UNIX Communications Facility

Managing

uucp

and Usenet

Tim O'Reilly and Grace Todino

O'Reilly & Associates, Inc.

Learning GNU Emacs

By Deb Cameron & Bill Rosenblatt

GNU Emacs is the most popular and widespread of the Emacs family of editors. It is also the most powerful and flexible. (Unlike all other text editors, GNU Emacs is a complete working environment—you can stay within Emacs all day without leaving.) This book tells you how to get started with the GNU Emacs editor. It will also "grow" with you: as you become more proficient, this book will help you learn how to use Emacs more effectively. It will take you from basic Emacs usage (simple text editing) to moderately complicated customization and programming.

The book is aimed at new Emacs users, whether or not they are programmers. Also useful for readers switching from other Emacs implementations to GNU Emacs.

442 pages, ISBN 0-937175-84-6

Learning the vi Editor

5th Edition
By Linda Lamb

For many users, working in the UNIX environment means using *vi*, a full-screen text editor available on most UNIX systems. Even those who know *vi* often make use of only a small number of its features. This is the complete guide to text editing with *vi*. Early chapters cover the basics; later chapters explain more advanced editing tools, such as *ex* commands and global search and replacement.

192 pages, ISBN 0-937175-67-6

Learning the UNIX Operating System

2nd Edition
By Grace Todino & John Strang

If you are new to UNIX, this concise introduction will tell you just what you need to get started, and no more. Why wade through a 600-page book when you can begin working productively in a matter of minutes?

Topics covered include:

• Logging in and logging out
• Managing UNIX files and directories
• Sending and receiving mail
• Redirecting input/output
• Pipes and filters
• Background processing
• Customizing your account

"If you have someone on your site who has never worked on a UNIX system and who needs a quick how-to, Nutshell has the right booklet. *Learning the UNIX Operating System* can get a newcomer rolling in a single session."—;login

84 pages, ISBN 0-937175-16-1

MH & xmh: E-mail for Users & Programmers

By Jerry Peek

Customizing your e-mail environment can save you time and make communicating more enjoyable. *MH & xmh: E-mail for Users and Programmers* explains how to use, customize, and program with the MH electronic mail commands, available on virtually any UNIX system. The handbook also covers *xmh*, an X Window System client that runs MH programs.

The basics are easy. But MH lets you do much more than what most people expect an e-mail system to be able to do. This handbook is packed with explanations and useful examples of MH features, some of which the standard MH documentation only hints at.

598 pages, ISBN 0-937175-63-3

UNIX Text Processing

Learning
GNU Emacs

Debra Cameron and Bill Rosenblatt
O'Reilly & Associates, Inc.

Guide to OSF/1: A Technical Synopsis

By O'Reilly & Associates Staff

OSF/1, Mach, POSIX, SVID, SVR4, X/Open, 4.4BSD, XPG, B-1 security, parallelization, threads, virtual file systems, shared libraries, streams, extensible loader, internationalization.... Need help sorting it all out? If so, then this technically competent introduction to the mysteries of the OSF/1 operating system is a book for you. In addition to its exposition of OSF/1, it offers a list of differences between OSF/1 and System V, Release 4 and a look ahead at what is coming in DCE.

This is not the usual O'Reilly how-to book. It will not lead you through detailed programming examples under OSF/1. Instead, it asks the prior question, What is the nature of the beast? It helps you figure out how to approach the programming task by giving you a comprehensive technical overview of the operating system's features and services, and by showing how they work together.

304 pages, ISBN 0-937175-78-1

POSIX Programmer's Guide

By Donald Lewine

Most UNIX systems today are POSIX-compliant because the Federal government requires it. Even OSF and UI agree on support for POSIX. However, given the manufacturer's documentation, it can be difficult to distinguish system-specific features from those features defined by POSIX.

The *POSIX Programmer's Guide*, intended as an explanation of the POSIX standard and as a reference for the POSIX.1 programming library, will help you write more portable programs. This guide is especially helpful if you are writing programs that must run on multiple UNIX platforms. This guide will also help you convert existing UNIX programs for POSIX-compliance.

640 pages, ISBN 0-937175-73-0

Managing NFS and NIS

By Hal Stern

A modern computer system that is not part of a network is an anomaly. But managing a network and getting it to perform well can be a problem. This book describes two tools that are absolutely essential to distributed computing environments: the Network Filesystem (NFS) and the Network Information System (formerly called the "yellow pages" or YP).

As popular as NFS is, it is a black box for most users and administrators. This book provides a comprehensive discussion of how to plan, set up, and debug an NFS network. It is the only book we're aware of that discusses NFS and network performance tuning. This book also covers the NFS automounter, network security issues, diskless workstations, and PC/NFS. It also tells you how to use NIS to manage your own database applications, ranging from a simple telephone list to controlling access to network services. If you are managing a network of UNIX systems, or are thinking of setting up a UNIX network, you can't afford to overlook this book.

436 pages, ISBN 0-937175-75-7

Power Programming with RPC

By John Bloomer

A distributed application is designed to access resources across a network. In a broad sense, these resources could be user input, a central database, configuration files, etc., that are distributed on various computers across the network rather than found on a single computer. RPC, or remote procedure calling, is the ability to distribute the execution of functions on remote computers outside of the application's current address space. This allows you to break large or complex programming problems into routines that can be executed independently of one another to take advantage of multiple computers. Thus, RPC makes it possible to attack a problem using a form of parallel or multi-processing.

Written from a programmer's perspective, this book shows what you can do with RPC and presents a framework for learning it.

494 pages, ISBN 0-937175-77-3

Practical C Programming

By Steve Oualline

There are lots of introductory C books, but this is the first one that has the no-nonsense, practical approach that has made Nutshell Handbooks famous. C programming is more than just getting the syntax right. Style and debugging also play a tremendous part in creating well-running programs.

Practical C Programming teaches you how to create programs that are easy to read, maintain and debug. Practical rules are stressed. For example, there are 15 precedence rules in C (&& comes before || comes before ?:). The practical programmer simplifies these down to two: 1) Multiply and divide come before addition and subtraction and 2) Put parentheses around everything else. Electronic Archaeology, the art of going through someone else's code, is also described.

Topics covered include:

• Good programming style

• C syntax: what to use and what not to use

• The programming environment, including *make*

• The total programming process

• Floating point limitations

• Tricks and surprises

Covers Turbo C (DOS) as well as the UNIX C compiler.

420 pages, ISBN 0-937175-65-X

Using C on the UNIX System

By Dave Curry

Using C on the UNIX System provides a thorough introduction to the UNIX system call libraries. It is aimed at programmers who already know C but who want to take full advantage of the UNIX programming environment. If you want to learn how to work with the operating system and if you want to write programs that can interact with directories, terminals and networks at the lowest level, you will find this book essential. It is impossible to write UNIX utilities of any sophistication without understanding the material in this book.

"A gem of a book. The author's aim is to provide a guide to system programming, and he succeeds admirably. His balance is steady between System V and BSD-based systems, so readers come away knowing both."
—SUN Expert

250 pages, ISBN 0-937175-23-4

Managing Projects with make

2nd Edition
By Steve Talbott and Andrew Oram

Make is one of UNIX's greatest contributions to software development, and this book is the clearest description of *make* ever written. Even the smallest software project typically involves a number of files that depend upon each other in various ways. If you modify one or more source files, you must relink the program after recompiling some, but not necessarily all, of the sources.

Make greatly simplifies this process. By recording the relationships between sets of files, *make* can automatically perform all the necessary updating. The new edition of this book describes all the basic features of *make* and provides guidelines on meeting the needs of large, modern projects.

152 pages, ISBN 0-937175-90-0

Checking C Programs with lint

By Ian F. Darwin

The *lint* program checker has proven itself time and again to be one of the best tools for finding portability problems and certain types of coding errors in C programs. *lint* verifies a program or program segments against standard libraries, checks the code for common portability errors, and tests the programming against some tried and true guidelines. linting your code is a necessary (though not sufficient) step in writing clean, portable, effective programs. This book introduces you to *lint*, guides you through running it on your programs and helps you to interpret *lint*'s output.

"Short, useful, and to the point. I recommend it for self-study to all involved with C in a UNIX environment."—Computing Reviews

84 pages, ISBN 0-937175-30-7

Programming with curses

By John Strang

curses is a UNIX library of functions for controlling a terminal's display screen from a C program. It can be used to provide a screen driver for a program (such as a visual editor) or to improve a program's user interface.

This handbook will help you make use of the *curses* library in your C programs. We have presented ample material on *curses* and its implementation in UNIX so that you understand the whole as well as its parts.

"You should rush right out and get a copy of both [both the *curses* and the *termcap* book]. Put your name all over them right away, because every programmer in the vicinity will try to steal them."—Message-ID: <398@minya.UUCP>

76 pages, ISBN 0-937175-02-1

sed & awk

By Dale Dougherty

For people who create and modify text files, *sed* and *awk* are power tools for editing. Most of the things that you can do interactively with a text editor. However, using *sed* and *awk* can save many hours of repetitive work in achieving the same result.

This book contains a comprehensive treatment of *sed* and *awk* syntax. Plus, it emphasizes the kinds of practical problems that *sed* and *awk* can help users to solve, with many useful example scripts and programs.

"*sed & awk* is a must for UNIX system programmers and administrators, and even general UNIX readers will benefit. I have over a hundred UNIX and C books in my personal library at home, but only a dozen are duplicated on the shelf where I work. This one just became number twelve."
—Root Journal

414 pages, ISBN 0-937175-59-5

Programming Perl

By Larry Wall & Randal Schwartz

This is the authoritative guide to the hottest new UNIX utility in years, co-authored by the creator of that utility.

Perl is a language for easily manipulating text, files and processes. Perl provides a more concise and readable way to do many jobs that were formerly accomplished (with difficulty) by programming in the C language or one of the shells. Even though Perl is not yet a standard part of UNIX, it is likely to be available wherever you choose to work. And if it isn't, you can get it and install it easily and free of charge.

482 pages, ISBN 0-937175-64-1

UNIX for FORTRAN Programmers

By Mike Loukides

UNIX for FORTRAN Programmers provides the serious scientific programmer with an introduction to the UNIX operating system and its tools. The intent of the book is to minimize the UNIX entry barrier: to familiarize readers with the most important tools so they can be productive as quickly as possible. *UNIX for FORTRAN Programmers* shows readers how to do things that they're interested in: not just how to use a tool like *make* or *rcs*, but how it is used in program development and fits into the toolset as a whole.

"An excellent book describing the features of the UNIX FORTRAN compiler f77 and related software. This book is extremely well written."
—American Mathematical Monthly

264 pages, ISBN 0-937175-51-X